"In the day and age of EdTPA assessments and innovative co-teaching approaches to internships, a book such as this one is essential for the effective mentorship of preservice teachers. No longer will 'mentors mentoring as they were mentored' be enough. The CARE model provides a practical approach, contextualized with theory and grounded in the contemporary realities of teacher education."

Janet Alsup, Purdue University, USA

"Timely, research-based, and practice-oriented, *Mentoring Preservice Teachers Through Practice* is a 'must have' for teacher educators involved in clinical practice and school-university partnerships. Wetzel, Hoffman, and Maloch embrace, rather than gloss over, the complexity of teaching and present a framework that helps mentor teachers and university facilitators support preservice teachers in clinical practice. Positioning teaching as a reflective activity, the Coaching with CARE framework helps preservice teachers, mentor teachers, and university teacher educators improve their craft by keeping the focus on students' learning."

Seth Parsons, George Mason University, USA

MENTORING PRESERVICE TEACHERS THROUGH PRACTICE

Supporting and challenging cooperating teachers to grow in their mentoring and coaching practices with preservice teachers and also in their own work as classroom teachers, this practical guide presents and illustrates the Coaching with CARE model—a framework for reflection and action that helps cultivate a perspective on teaching that puts students at the center of teacher preparation and places value on apprenticeship and participation in learning. The CARE model takes a turn away from traditional evaluation-based "training" approaches, offering a way for cooperating teachers, and facilitators and university teacher educators who work with them, to come together to shape innovative coaching and mentoring experiences for preservice teachers.

Mentoring Preservice Teachers Through Practice, building on the authors' own work with cooperating teachers, is based on the most recent research on learning to teach and supporting preservice teachers and grounded in the realities of teacher education today. Each chapter includes questions for discussion and suggested readings that can be used to explore the focus of the chapter more deeply as well as relevant research reports published by the authors.

Melissa Mosley Wetzel is Associate Professor of Language and Literacy in the Department of Curriculum and Instruction at The University of Texas at Austin, USA.

James V. Hoffman is Professor of Language and Literacy Studies in the Department of Curriculum and Instruction at The University of Texas at Austin, USA.

Beth Maloch is Professor of Language and Literacy Studies in the Department of Curriculum and Instruction and Associate Dean of Teacher Education, Student Affairs, and Administration for the College of Education at The University of Texas at Austin, USA.

MENTORING PRESERVICE TEACHERS THROUGH PRACTICE

A Framework for Coaching with CARE

Melissa Mosley Wetzel, James V. Hoffman, and Beth Maloch

Routledge
Taylor & Francis Group

NEW YORK AND LONDON

First published 2017
by Routledge
711 Third Avenue, New York, NY 10017

and by Routledge
2 Park Square, Milton Park, Abingdon, Oxon, OX14 4RN

Routledge is an imprint of the Taylor & Francis Group, an informa business

© 2017 Taylor & Francis

Library of Congress Cataloguing in Publication Data
Names: Mosley Wetzel, Melissa, author. | Hoffman, James V. | Maloch, Beth.
Title: Mentoring preservice teachers through practice : a framework for
coaching with CARE / by Melissa Mosley Wetzel, James V. Hoffman, Beth
Maloch.
Description: New York : Routledge, 2017. | Includes bibliographical
references and index.
Identifiers: LCCN 2016051713| ISBN 9781138697836 (hardback) |
ISBN 9781138697843 (pbk.)
Subjects: LCSH: Student teachers—Training of. | Mentoring in education.
Classification: LCC LB2157 .M67 2017 | DDC 371.102—dc23
LC record available at https://lccn.loc.gov/2016051713

ISBN: 978-1-138-69783-6 (hbk)
ISBN: 978-1-138-69784-3 (pbk)
ISBN: 978-1-315-52053-7 (ebk)

Typeset in Bembo
by diacriTech, Chennai

CONTENTS

PREFACE

Each year in the United States, over 80,000 elementary teachers complete their student teaching experience in university-based preparation programs. An equal, or even greater number, are working in other kinds of practicum/classroom experiences that are part of the same teacher preparation programs. The research around the work in practicum experiences has revealed a number of important findings. First, these experiences are the most important in a teacher education program in shaping the learning of the preservice teacher. Second, in many institutions, there is minimal participation of university faculty in the design or offering of these experiences. Third, the cooperating teacher is the primary mediator for the practicum experience in the classroom. Fourth, the cooperating teacher has been given little preparation or guidance in how to support the preservice teachers. Fifth, and finally, in the absence of any guidance the cooperating teacher tends to rely on the same kind of evaluative model of support that they received in their teacher preparation program and that they continue to receive in their schools. The status quo is preserved. We can do better. This book represents our work to build partnerships and a shared model of teacher development among the partners who work with preservice teachers—university professors and field supervisors, schools and cooperating teachers, all in the interest of the preservice teachers we hope to serve better.

This book has grown out of our program of research into preservice teacher preparation within a mentoring and coaching model called Coaching with CARE. We began our project in 2012 when we designed a Master's Program in Mentoring, Leadership, and Professional Development at the University of Texas at Austin. We provided financial support for our first three cohorts of cooperating teachers to pursue their degrees while working alongside our preservice teachers in their classrooms. We owe a great deal of gratitude to those brilliant teachers who helped us develop the model of Coaching with CARE. We also studied the process, using a development and design-based research model. For the last two years, we have continued this work with a larger group of teachers through a professional development program. Each year, we engage in learning alongside about 35 area teachers who want to know more about teaching, learning, and mentoring. The book is based on the findings from our research, but we have composed it as a guide to understanding and implementing the model.

The audience for this book is teachers who serve as mentors for preservice teachers working in classrooms—whom we call "cooperating teachers" in this book, and in addition, those university-based field supervisors who often work with preservice teachers around their practice in their field-placement classrooms. Together, university faculty and cooperating teachers can use this book to shape innovative coaching and mentoring experiences for preservice teachers. Our goal with this book is to disrupt this status quo of a separation between those who hold a stake in teacher preparation. We have worked in close collaboration to develop a model of coaching that, we believe, can be transformative in initial teacher preparation and beyond.

Mentoring Preservice Teachers Through Practice is structured in four parts. **Part I, Teacher Preparation: The Practice Turn in Teacher Education,** provides the reader with a background for work with the Coaching with CARE model. Chapter 1 introduces the notion that we are always becoming—on a pathway to knowing more, doing better—because we are human and because we are teachers. We follow this introductory chapter with Chapter 2, a chapter that asks the reader to engage in their process of becoming a coach, a mentor, and a teacher, continuing the theme of "becoming." Next, Chapter 3 focuses on how we situate our work in teacher education—namely within the practice turn in teacher education away from a competency view rooted in behaviorism to a practice view that places value on apprenticeship and participation in learning. Voices of teachers we have worked with are woven through each chapter in Part I.

In **Part II, The Coaching with CARE Model and Cycle,** Chapters 4–7 focus on the CARE model and provide the resources and tools of coaching. Chapter 4 is an overview of the model, and in this chapter we deconstruct the acronym of CARE, and provide a theoretical rationale for each dimension. Chapter 5 is the first chapter in which we provide practical tools for entering into reflective cycles with the preservice teacher. We introduce the ideas of Activity Configurations and Purposeful Observations—two of the ways we prepare preservice teachers for a reflective teaching practice. Chapters 6 and 7 focus on the four-part cycle of pre-conference, observation, post-conference and planning, the heart of the CARE model. In each of the chapters, but particularly in Chapters 6 and 7, we provide longer transcripts of coaching conversations along with our deconstructions of those conversations, in order to support you in seeing and hearing this model in action.

In **Part III, The Three C's of CARE: Community, Critical, and Content,** Chapters 8 and 9 are focused on the "what" of coaching—what are the topics and concerns that we might address through a coaching model. In Chapter 8 we address classroom communities and critical issues in coaching, and reframe many of the conversations that might occur about management as conversations about communities and critical social issues. Chapter 9 emerged from our interviews with content experts in our field, and in this chapter, we work to make sense of the ways that pedagogical content knowledge is constructed through coaching across different domains, as well as the connections between those domains.

In **Part IV, Expanding Tools for Coaching,** we provide two extensions of the model, Collaborative Coaching (Chapter 10) and Retrospective Video Analysis (Chapter 11); two ways of extending the practice we have developed through our design-based research. Each chapter also includes a case study, in which we draw on teacher voices to illustrate dimensions of coaching within the CARE model. We complete Part IV with Conclusions (Chapter 12). In this chapter, we revisit the underpinnings of the CARE model and we return to the notion of communities of coaches. Each of the parts of this book represents theory and practice, and the book was designed to be read from start to end.

This book will be useful to any professional development program. In our own teacher preparation program, we have designed a 12-session professional development program, and each session aligns with one chapter of the book. We envision using the book across one year, while the cooperating and preservice teachers are working together. Along with Parts II and IV of the book, the cooperating teachers might video record their own coaching sessions and work with others to coach one another around their practice. We call this work "coaching the coach," and we draw on the exact same model of reflective work that we use with the preservice teachers. Applying notions of CARE to work with peers is both enlightening and deepens one's understanding of the model.

ACKNOWLEDGMENTS

We would like to first recognize the team of graduate students at The University of Texas at Austin who have been working on the Coaching with CARE project since 2012. Laura Taylor, Alina Adonyi Pruitt, Erin Greeter, Samuel Dejulio, Saba Khan Vlach, Natalie Svrcek, Charlotte Land, Kira Lee Keenan, Catherine Lammert, and Cori Salmeron—your thinking and contributions are all part of this book. In particular, we would like to thank and acknowledge the contributions of Natalie Svrcek and Saba Khan Vlach for their work as research assistants in preparation of this book manuscript. We would also like to express deep gratitude to over 70 participants who worked with us as cooperating teachers, preservice teachers, and field supervisors. Because our project was a design and development study, the model grew and developed because you used it. We are thankful and appreciative for each of you and your participation. Finally, we would like to thank both the Spencer Foundation and the Association of Literacy Educators and Researchers (ALER) for your generous support of our work. And, without the support of the College of Education and the Department of Curriculum at the University of Texas, this work would not have been possible.

PART I

Teacher Preparation

The Practice Turn in Teacher Education

1

UNFINISHED AND BECOMING

"I am a teacher educator." Say that aloud. It doesn't just roll off the tongue in the same way as saying "I am a teacher." You aspire to become a mentor of preservice teachers. You are embarking on a journey that will be both familiar and different. You will be challenged along the way and in these challenges you will find opportunities for growth. Whether you are working as a university-based teacher educator, a mentor of a new teacher in a school, or with a group of teachers in a peer support learning community, you are trying out and trying on a new teacher educator identity. You will have to construct your identity for yourself. The identity of teacher educator doesn't come in a degree or a certification. The identity of teacher educator comes with time and hard work making sense of practice. There are no shortcuts. Even this book is, at best, a meager starting point for your journey. You will take on the responsibility of becoming.

Mentor teachers are individuals who take on the responsibility of guiding and supporting preservice teachers as they develop practical knowledge for teaching. We, the authors of this book, have been investigating possibilities around the support mentor teachers offer to new teachers that taken us far beyond the traditional. We resist the notion that effective teaching can be represented in a set of discrete competencies arrayed along a hierarchical sequence from the simple to the complex. We resist the notion that the role of the teacher educator is to install these competencies into preservice teachers' behaviors at a mastery level to get them ready to teach. This "training" model for teacher education that focuses almost exclusively on the procedural and technical is fundamentally flawed and has corrupted efforts to provide support that matters for growth. The training model for teacher education ignores the cognitive, social, emotional, and moral demands of teaching. The training model for teacher education has failed in educating teachers in the same ways that the "banking" model for classroom teaching—the idea that teachers make "deposits" into passive students' minds—has failed to meet student needs (Freire, 1970). Rather, Freire proposed that dialogue, which requires (1) humility, (2) hope, (3) faith, (4) love, and (5) critical thinking, is a pathway to better and more powerful approaches for nurturing teacher growth and promoting a professional identity that can thrive in the face of adversity or challenges.

The key question we address in this book as teacher educators **is not,** "How do we get teachers to perform in a certain way?" Nor is our key question, "How do we give teachers the knowledge they need to know to be effective?" Our key question as teacher educators is: "How do we support preservice teachers along a path to becoming the teachers they aspire to become?" This is not a single path, and there won't be one path for everyone. We embrace diversity, creativity, and possibility in practice in ways that push back against the norms for a standardized or normalized ways of being a teacher. The more different we are, the greater the possibilities for us to learn from each other. And, because of our differences, we will support teachers on their path differently. We strive for aspiring teachers to become knowledgeable, thoughtfully adaptive teachers (Fairbanks et al., 2009) who recognize that the practice of teaching is always responsive to the students they serve and the contexts in which they work in the moment—not the districts, administrators, states, nor institutions they serve.

Coaching is the primary focus for our work but it is only one of the things that mentors do with their preservice teachers. In our work, we draw on models of coaching that emphasize participation and collaboration. We see "trying out" and "trying on," or what Grossman (2011) describes as "approximations" of practice, as the necessary contexts for preservice teachers to become thoughtfully adaptive, critical, and independent learners through practice. Often, the field experience is seen only as a place to apply pedagogy, and the mentor is expected to provide direct feedback and judge whether the teacher has done it the "right" way. Rather, we see these practice contexts as times when the identity of teachers is fundamentally shaped, and therefore, these authentic experiences in practice must be accompanied by attention to and reflection on the work that preservice teachers do. We must attend to approximations and the changes that are made in practice and after practice in order to respond to students. When these conditions are in place, novices learn that their students are their teachers for life when the teacher's role is to attend to what students are saying, doing, and feeling. The mentor teacher is the person who can support the aspiring teacher by becoming their companion on a journey of learning.

Our Teacher Preparation Program

Our work around mentoring and coaching has been focused at the elementary level on the work of mentor teachers working in the role of cooperating teachers in a university-based teacher education program. While this focus has been on preservice teachers, we see these same practices as useful when mentor teachers support beginning teachers through their first years of teaching. Indeed, we see the practices we describe as adaptable to the context of peer coaching among experienced teachers.

At our university, the teacher preparation program is a large program; we graduate around 300 teachers every year. Each student is placed in a cohort that has about 20–25 students and travels through a three-semester program together. Coursework sits alongside field experiences, because the research about teacher education that we lean on has told us that the ways that coursework is integrated with field experiences matter. When our students are in one place, we want them thinking about the other place. We want them to question into the coursework and field experiences because they have these two side-by-side experiences.

The CARE model, which we will explore in this book, has expanded the ways we work with preservice teachers throughout our preparation programs. Thus far, we have worked with cooperating teachers in our elementary preparation program and are beginning to work with secondary English education cooperating teachers. We are fortunate for the opportunities we have to work directly with these cooperating teachers, and we are always looking to expand even further what we do.

In our research over the last five years, we have seen the power of bringing the cooperating teacher front and center in the community of teacher preparation. We take the long view in teacher preparation. In making program decisions we have not chosen the easy or efficient path. Reflective coaching is difficult and time intensive but worth the effort. In the last chapter of this book, we return to the ways that CARE is infused throughout our program.

Who Are We?

We, the three authors of this book, are experienced elementary teachers. We now serve in the role of university-based teacher educators with a specialization in language and literacy studies. We work both in the preparation of elementary teachers as well as in graduate programs for master's and doctoral students. We have been working over the years to design and implement a teacher education program that is on the cutting edge of research and practice.

We are literacy educators, but we are teachers first, and we focus on general principles of teaching practice and teacher development. At the same time, we understand that different disciplines in teaching have different structures and histories that are important to understand. There may be common features of coaching across disciplines, but there also may be different, specific practices that a mentor might use in mathematics, science, or social studies, which we will address in Chapter 9.

Our research is our practice. We subscribe to Kurt Lewin's (1951) notion that there is "nothing as practical as a good theory" (p. 169). We extend this position with our own spin to argue that there is "nothing as theoretical as good practice."

In writing this book, we endeavor to speak to practice directly with concrete examples drawing from our experiences. We put the "academic" discourse in places that can be used as a resource for digging deeper into the scholarly literature around the issues of coaching and mentoring. Throughout this book we will suggest readings to extend your learning. You will meet many of the outstanding preservice teachers, cooperating teachers, and researchers who have been and continue to be our companions throughout this inquiry. Their voices will be found in almost every chapter.

Although our focus in this book is toward developing your role in supporting preservice teachers, everything we address will, at the same time, be around who you are a as classroom teacher in this moment and in the future. Dialogue is central to both activities. The ways in which we engage with novices in our words and actions will spill back into our thinking about how we engage with the learners in our own classrooms. The act of mentoring or coaching a novice is not an altogether altruistic endeavor of "giving" to the profession. Your experiences in mentoring in coaching will change you, for the better, as a classroom teacher and as a person. We subscribe to Paulo Freire's (1970/1995) belief that we are better as educators to position ourselves as problem posers rather than problem solvers. He writes:

> Problem-posing education affirms [people] as beings in the process of becoming—as unfinished, incomplete beings in and with a likewise unfinished reality ... The unfinished character of [people] and the transformational character of reality necessitate that education be an ongoing activity. (p. 65)

The CARE model is unfinished. We are all unfinished. We are all becoming. We will present ideas that challenge all of us to change. We are not about preparing teachers to fit into something that exists. That would be easy for all parties and is the status quo in many teacher education programs. We aim to prepare teachers who can make schools better places for learning for all. You will likely become very uncomfortable in the process as you are asked to let go of some beliefs about teaching that have been instilled through your many years of exposure to teaching as a student in schools (what was termed by Lortie [1975] the "apprenticeship of observation") and through your experiences as a teacher in schools.

A Case: A Place of Uncertainty

In each chapter of this book, we will draw from the voices of the teachers we have worked with over five years of exploring the CARE model within this teacher preparation program. Denise is a cooperating teacher who worked with us during the second year of this project. Denise had worked as a coach and mentor to preservice teachers for six years before joining our graduate program. She admitted early on that change was hard for her, and she had developed a reputation as an expert teacher in her school and district, which she did not want to disrupt. It felt unsafe for Denise to share her vulnerability as she learned about reflective coaching and CARE. Like so many cooperating teachers, Denise shared that her preparation to serve as a coach and mentor came in the form of reading a PowerPoint from her district, and she believed that it was her job to provide direct feedback and evaluate the preservice teacher's performance. After one semester of working with the CARE model with the support of her colleagues at the university, Denise's thinking had evolved, and she was ready to move forward as a learner and problem-poser with her preservice teacher. Denise expressed her thoughts in her class' blog,

> There is still so much for me to learn and I am still in a place of uncertainty— and I don't really like it that much. I would be lying if I said that this was an easy semester for me. Everything that I have thought, felt as a teacher has been somewhat challenged and I now stand on a rug of discomfort but I know that that ground will become more stable as we continue on the journey [Blog Post, December 2013].

Denise proclaimed her "uncertain" state with hesitation; however, with the support of her learning community, she was willing to accept that teaching (and teachers) could not remain in a static state. Tensions with your own belief systems will surely rise up. Struggle is essential to learning. But you do not need to take this journey on your own. In fact, we encourage you to find colleagues to grow with you.

In this book, we feature our own teacher preparation program and the teachers who have worked beside us to construct this model of CARE. You also are working with teacher educators who are as committed as we are in preparing the preservice teachers they work with, and in choosing to use this text, you and these partners, perhaps are beginning to move down this challenging and exciting path of coaching with CARE. We encourage you to read and engage with the ideas we present in this book with others who are on a similar journey, a critical friend, an inquiry group, or an academic course. Your learning community will be an important interpretive and support base for your growth. In each chapter, we provide some suggestions to guide your conversations. We are excited for the opportunity to join with you in this journey.

Some Thinking and Talking To Do

- Think about how it once felt to be a novice teacher, in your own student teaching experience. How do you feel about being a new teacher educator? Are there any parallels between who you are, reading this book, and that experience of being a new teacher?

- Where have you encountered the ideas of thoughtfully adaptive teaching, approximations in teaching, or problem-posing education before in your own development as a teacher, and what questions do you have about these three foundational processes? What might these ideas have to do with being a cooperating teacher?

References

Fairbanks, C. M., Duffy, G. G., Faircloth, B. S., He, Y., Levin, B., Rohr, J., and Stein, C. (2009). Beyond knowledge: Exploring why some teachers are more thoughtfully adaptive than others. *Journal of Teacher Education*, 61(1–2), 161–71.

Freire, P. (1970). *Pedagogy of the oppressed*. (M. B. Ramos, Trans.). New York, NY: Bloomsbury. (Original work published in 1968).

Grossman, P. (2011). Framework for teaching practice: A brief history of an idea. *Teachers College Record*, 113(12), 2836–43.

Lewin, K. (1951). *Field theory in social science: Selected theoretical papers*. D. Cartwright (Ed.). New York, NY: Harper and Row.

Lortie, D. C. and Clement, D. (1975). *Schoolteacher: A sociological study*. Chicago, IL: University of Chicago Press.

2

A MENTOR, A COACH, A TEACHER

Who Are You? Who Are You Becoming?

Jane, one of the cooperating teachers we have worked with for many years, has taught us much about being a mentor, a coach, and a teacher. She was in the first cohort of our master's program and we have come to think of our CARE model as informed by the ways she and her cohort appropriated the model and gave it shape through their practice. We begin each section with her words—her image of what it means to *become* through these different roles, and end with a case of the dialogue between her and the preservice teacher who worked with her that first year.

Mentor: Who Gets To Be a Mentor? What Does a Mentor Do?

Different preservice teachers are on different points on the continuum of needs, level of comfort, and have different skill sets. Responsive mentoring requires us all to be observant and make a real effort to get to know all we can about our student teacher so we can mentor effectively.

Historically, "mentor" has been used to describe someone who is trusted and faithful as an advisor and protector—usually around entering some new practice or role. Artists, scientists, doctors, and lawyers typically have mentoring relationships in their past that supported some critical transitions. The root meaning of the term "mentor" is found in Greek mythology. Mentor was a friend of Odysseus, who he entrusted to look after his son, Telemachus, when he set out on his journey to fight in the Trojan War. When the goddess Athena would visit Telemachus, she would take on the disguise of Mentor. Telemachus was unaware that he had more than one Mentor to guide him.

Mentoring is oriented toward the whole person during a time of change. Mentoring cannot take place in the absence of a personal relationship of trust. Expertise is certainly an important resource for a mentor, but the social and emotional work of mentoring is just as important. A mentoring relationship can emerge informally in a context and often may not even be labeled as a mentoring relationship. The novice selects a mentor based on qualities of respect, admiration, and inspiration. There may be some expression of the desired relationship. "I want you to mentor me." Most often, though, the relationship grows in working together in some shared space.

Think of someone in your life experience, not just in teaching, who has been a mentor to you. How did you enter into that relationship? What was the need you were acting on? How did that relationship grow over time? What work was involved in building that relationship?

Challenges In Being a Mentor

In education, the construct of a mentor has become highly proceduralized. Typically, you do not seek out a mentor. You are assigned one. For preservice teachers, this is the cooperating teacher. For novice teachers, this is likely another teacher in the school who teaches a similar content or level. All of these assignments are made with the best of intentions and in many, many cases the trusting, inspiring, and admiring parts of the relationship grow into fruition. When these relationships don't grow, the novice teacher might be fortunate in establishing informal mentoring relationships with other teachers who satisfy their needs.

As with so many phenomena today, the term mentor more often than not appears as a verb rather than a noun. "I mentor my student teacher." The movement into a verb has placed the relationship qualities of a mentor into the background and foregrounds a set of things that are done to someone. We prefer to think of a mentor as a term that describes someone who is in a relationship with another person and taking on a particular set of responsibilities. The acts of a mentor should be described for the form they take and the purposes they serve. "I'm trying to help my Angela understand how our grade level team works" (i.e., the norms and expectations for participation within that group). "I'm spending a lot of time with Adriane just walking around the neighborhood and getting comfortable with the home and community environment of our school." These kinds of moves are as much about building trust and confidence as they are about passing on some skill or strategy.

There is also something to be troubled around the word "my" in describing the mentor role as well. Is there really possession, power, or exclusion that we intend when we say "She is my mentee"? The use of "my" presupposes an identity that may not be all that healthy in building a relationship. "Grace is doing her student teaching experience in our classroom." The use of "our" plays forward in many positive ways that "my" does not.

How Do You Build Trust with the Person You Are Working with?

Trust is essential in growing into teaching. Without trust there will be no risk-taking. Without risk-taking there will be no growth. There is nothing magical here or any kind of formula. It is not unlike the relationship you build with the students in your classroom. Each child is different and each child moves into a trusting relationship with her teacher and with her classmates in different ways and at different paces. Figure 2.1 provides a few recommendations for you to consider (and expand on!) as you consider establishing a trusting relationship such as sharing both professionally and personally with each other, creating a safe environment, and making time for your relationship to grow.

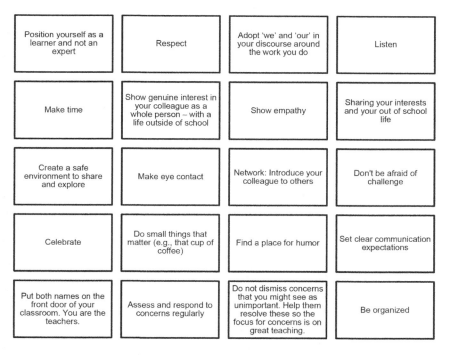

FIGURE 2.1 Recommendations for Establishing a Trusting Relationship with Your Preservice Teacher

Coach: Who Gets To Be a Coach? What Does a Coach Do?

She [the preservice teacher] and I were having a conference, post-lesson, and I was using some coaching strategies; I was getting her to point out different things instead of telling her what I saw. I said, "I noticed that you did _____; did you plan it?" I asked, "Why did you do that, and what message do you think the kids took away?" She was searching, uncomfortable, and you could tell that she really felt like she wanted to hear what I thought. I almost broke! But, I didn't. I'm hoping that's a beginning step and as we move forward it will get better.

When many hear the word "coach," they think of a person who trains an athlete. A coach might also make decisions about how the team plays during games. Today, the term coach has been appropriated into a wide variety of contexts including "life coaches," "career coaches," and "relationship coaches." We also see more and more the term "coach" to describe teachers working with teachers in schools across the country across many of the academic disciplines (e.g., literacy coaches and mathematics coaches).

On the positive side, the appropriation of the coaching metaphor has brought support into the context of practice. Coaches work with teachers in classrooms around teaching. However, there are some negatives associated with the term coaching:

A focus on behavior. Athletic coaches focus a great deal on behaviors (e.g., motions, movement, technique) more than anything. We worry, with the coaching metaphor, that teaching is reduced to behaviors and that the mental and emotional work of teachers is ignored.

A power relationship. Athletic coaches are in charge. They run the team. They define what is desirable and what is not. We worry, with the coaching metaphor, that the teacher is positioned as someone who is told what to do not as someone constructing practice that is helpful to students.

A reductionist view of learning. Athletic coaches often break things down into small skill sets so the work can be concentrated and mastery of skills insured. We worry, with the coaching metaphor, that teachers will be asked to work in a decontextualized fashion rather than embracing the constant complexity of teaching.

The No Child Left Behind Act and Reading First program promoted the use of coaches in schools in a manner and to a degree that was unheard of in the past. Schools and districts were asked to choose and implement programs for students that had been validated through scientific processes. These programs would work only if they were implemented by teachers in classrooms with a high degree of fidelity. The term "fidelity" took on a very technical meaning in this context. Teachers were told they must do exactly what the program required without deviations or adjustments. If there was a script, then say it. If there were steps to follow, follow them.

Reading First coaches took on the dual role of monitor and supporter of implementation. The coach had an observation checklist, and this checklist reflected the high fidelity version of the program. The observed teacher would be given feedback based on their performance and areas that needed to change in order for there to be fidelity to the program. Coaching was about compliance.

This version of coaching is the polar opposite of what we will advocate for in this book and explain in the coming chapters. Our rejection of this "fidelity" (or what we will term as "evaluative") model rests on many different areas of concern. First, fidelity is a questionable idea in teaching. One of the strongest qualities of effective teachers is their ability to adapt their teaching in the moment based on the ongoing assessments that are part of all instruction. Teachers thoughtfully adapt instruction based on need (e.g., something isn't working) or on opportunity (e.g., "I hadn't planned on going there but we can."). Coaching for fidelity constrains these essential acts of teaching. The fidelity model ignores research that shows that effective programs are modified in context for the learners. Second, this model positions the coach in power over the teacher. This power dynamic will never work for growth. The teacher needs to be in the lead, and the coach needs to be there not to evaluate but to help them make sense of their experiences and grow. In this power relationship the teacher is being manipulated by praise and the potential for rewards by conforming to the expectations of the more powerful. Third, fidelity is locked into a behavioral and performance view of teaching. The checklists are always about "doing" not about thinking. The checklists are typically focused on the teacher and not on the students. Fourth, deficit models of coaching are far less powerful than appreciative models. Fidelity coaching is all about fixing the things you didn't do. This, sadly, is a view that drives so much of classroom teaching. We fix teachers by filling in the gaps in what they know and do. The alternative, to identify what teachers are doing and attempting to do that is showing positive results with the students, is to scaffold on top of success.

The evaluative coaching model dominates education—not because it is better for teachers and students but because it serves an educational system that is oriented toward accountability and efficiency. Under the fidelity model everyone, including the coaches, are clearly accountable for what they do. The coach doesn't need any specialized knowledge of teaching or academic disciplines. The coach, like the teacher, just needs to be able to follow a script.

Our version of coaching is much more about creating a dialogue that supports growth as opposed to a script to follow. Returning to the opening quote, Jane proposed the idea of "coaching strategies" that allowed the preservice teacher to talk through what happened in the lesson. She indicates struggle—rather than evaluate, she asked the preservice teacher to think through the work. Her comment, "I almost broke" reminds us that coaching in this way is hard work! It asks us to think differently about the role of the coach as one who invites reflection through dialogue.

The model of coaching we will advocate for is one of making our thinking visible, as Jane reminds us:

I know we can't always give a play-by-play of our decisions every moment as we teach, but being aware of opportunities for team-teaching (even if it is impromptu) or those moments for them to "lean in" as we confer with readers and writers, settle down a dispute, or even coaching children through problem-solving is meaningful. We don't always know when something is going to happen or even what the result will be, but being aware of opportunities for teachable moments can provide a chance for making our thinking visible.

Teacher: Who Gets To Be a Teacher? What Does a Teacher Do?

I'm just thinking about over time—I've had quite a few student teachers, and they're not children, but it's just like the students in your classroom. They have different needs and different areas where they excel and kind of trying to watch them in such a way that you're able to lift them when they're ready is important, than trying to be the same way for each student teacher.

You are a teacher. At any moment in your life as a coach when you feel lost or confused about what is best in the moment to do or try, trust the teacher instincts in you. Coaching and teaching are different in who is served, but in almost every other way they are tied to the same identity. One of the most important things you can offer those you coach is for them to step inside of your teacher identity. We will rely heavily in this book on some strategies for you to be observed by the person you are coaching. This is kind of a role reversal exercise. You let the preservice teacher see into your teacher mind. All of this demands that you are both secure in the teacher you are becoming and open to reflection.

The coaching model we advocate is very much in line with a teacher who values thoughtfully adaptive teaching in her own practices. We have found that teachers with this mindset about their own teaching fall quite naturally into the coaching model. For teachers who come with a more traditional orientation toward teaching as imparting information, some of what we will ask of you in the coaching model will be difficult. Our experience in our research has been that teachers who struggle with the coaching model in this way often come to rethink their own teaching practices.

If you are working with preservice or novice teachers in your coaching, don't assume that they are blank slates. Individuals enter teaching through, what Lortie (1975) called, the "apprenticeship of observation." They know much about teaching through the 10,000 plus hours they have spent as a student in classrooms. They have internalized a way of thinking about what counts and what does not count as teaching. You can expect that their notions of what it means to teach, what feedback should look like, what praise should be given and when, and what control of the classroom means are very well established. A good part of what you will be doing is trying to replace this ingrained experiential model with a new one—in a very short amount of time.

Talk with your preservice teacher about teachers they remember who have been "outside the box," "against the grain," and "inspirational." What lasting impact did these teachers have on them? How can they take these examples from their lives and build on them?

Vision

A vision for teaching is a very personal construction of why we teach and what we hope for our students. Many people enter teaching because they like to be around kids. They have a lot of experience in working with kids in many different settings. These are nice places to start and it is hard to imagine a successful teacher who does not like being around kids. But, these are not sufficient reasons to teach in the face of the workload and time commitments, the pressure from just about every direction, the emotional responses required in teaching. What is it that centers a teacher in ways that they carry forward with the goal of serving students' academic, social, and emotional lives?

These are questions or conversations that you must be prepared to have with your preservice teacher. You need to have articulated your philosophy or vision of teaching in ways that you can share. You need to work with him or her to help them as they figure out this teaching thing in their lives.

Role Conflicts and Uncertainty

Telemachus never knew exactly who was giving him advice and counsel. Was it Mentor, his father's trusted friend? Was it the goddess Athena speaking through Mentor? A preservice or novice teacher might well look at her mentor and ask, "Who is talking to me now? Is it the voice of my friend and colleague? Or is the voice of authority and evaluation?"

The simultaneous identity/roles of mentor, coach, and teacher are necessary and mostly compatible. But there may come times of conflict as well. There is always the potential for tension and even contradiction. You are observing a science lesson being led by your student teacher. The discussion goes in a direction where the student teacher is presenting explanations that are incorrect. What do you do? Step in and take over the lesson? Stay out and hope you can fix things later? There is no simple answer. This is a tension in your responsibilities as a teacher to your students and as a coach to your preservice teacher.

At some point in the semester, perhaps, there may be an expectation that you will assign a grade to your student teacher that will possibly affect graduation, certification, and job search success. How do you step out of your role as mentor and into the role of evaluator? We have no answers to these questions and a lot will depend on context. In some mentoring and coaching contexts with novice teachers there is never a time when you are asked to evaluate.

To complicate this situation even further, you are not the only person involved with your preservice teacher. There are university professors, field supervisors, course instructors, principals, and many others. How are these voices being synchronized or is everyone on their own track?

Our point in raising these questions at the end of this chapter is to be consistent in our message that there is uncertainty and negotiation around everything we do in teaching and coaching. For now, our advice is to resist the simple answer (e.g., "Well, I would step in of course!") and consider everything around your new roles and the decisions you are making as you enter this triad of roles: mentor, coach, and teacher.

A Case: Dialogue

Before we conclude this chapter, we want to share a sample of dialogue between Jane and a preservice teacher, Stephanie. Recall Jane was in our first master's program cohort. This exchange took place during Stephanie's student teaching semester, and she was debriefing with Jane during their post-conference on a lesson she had taught during writing workshop. The children were working on writing "How-To" texts, and Jane shared how she noticed the students working together during their independent writing time. Please consider in what ways does Jane enact Freire's five ideas (humility, hope, faith, love, and critical thinking) in her talk. As you read the following excerpt, we also ask you to note why these ideas and dispositions might be important.

> **Jane:** I noticed.... Of course this has nothing to do with your lesson but everything to do with the freedom that you're giving them as writers.... The freedom that you were giving them to talk, and to share with one another, and they are completely—they seem in tune with what one another—what they're doing. Did anyone have a particular struggle with this concept?
>
> **Stephanie:** It was hard for them, some of them to decipher between this mini-lesson focused on "helpful hints" and the one I did previously on "cautionary message." Like with Carly and her cartwheel, she made sure to put that on the cover, "You should do this. You should not do this, like if you have a broken bone." Or just the helpful hint is, "You don't have to be on the grass. You can be on concrete."
>
> **Jane:** I've never, when I've done my "How-Tos," have introduced "cautionary message" or the "helpful hints," and so I'm wondering if you can talk a little bit about how you honed in on that. What did you see in their writing that made you choose these?
>
> **Stephanie:** It started I guess with Jason and Brian, when doing their conferences, and he was saying, "I'm doing this with a kindergartener; they're

going to have trouble. I should probably add this to my writing." I thought maybe this would be a good tool for some of them to add because some of them, I could see what they were trying to say, but I know if someone else, a kindergartener, was reading it, they might have a hard time, that would be an extra detail to add.

Jane: So you can just see how writer's workshop, it changes all the time and you're being responsive to what you're hearing and seeing in the classroom, and so the children are picking up on that as well.

In this exchange, Jane and Stephanie kept their dialogue centered on students and the moves that students were making as writers and collaborators. Jane was genuinely intrigued by Stephanie's observations of the students as they worked, and she recognized that Stephanie was making her teaching decisions based on what she saw and heard the students do and say. Jane used the word "responsive" to describe Stephanie's teaching, and as we can see from their turn-taking, Jane and Stephanie were both equally engaged in dialogue with each other.

Some Thinking and Talking To Do

- Who have been the mentors in your life and in what areas? What are the qualities that were most meaningful around your relationship? Who claimed whom in the mentoring relationship?
- Have you ever been coached in athletics? Thinking along the lines of a Venn diagram, what do teachers and coaches have in common and how is each different?
- What is your vision for teaching? How has this vision helped sustain you in the face of difficult circumstances in teaching? Can you talk about the biggest test you have had to face in your journey into teaching?
- Have you ever experienced a program change that was approached from a "fidelity" perspective? What was that experience like for you?
- How are accountability and efficiency dangerous concepts in education? What would happen if we substituted "responsibility" for the word "accountability" every time we encountered the word? How would our conversations be different? What would happen if we resisted the press for efficiency in teaching by saying "We'll just take as much time as we need." How would our conversations be different?
- How would you approach role conflicts in your mentoring and coaching work? How would you prepare yourself and those you work with in negotiating the difficult territories?
- Who else is involved in the support of your preservice or novice teacher? What is your relationship with them? How are you working together? How are you working separately?

- Why might the five ideas that Freire (1970) proposes as essential for dialogue be important? How do you achieve (1) humility, (2) hope, (3) faith, (4) love, and (5) critical thinking in a dialogic relationship?
- Are you ready to invest what is needed in time and energy into the mentoring and coaching of a new teacher? Why?

References

Freire, P. (1970). *Pedagogy of the oppressed*. (M. B. Ramos, Trans.). New York, NY: Continuum. (Original work published in 1968).
Lortie, D. C. and Clement, D. (1975). *Schoolteacher: A sociological study*. Chicago, IL: University of Chicago Press.

3

CHANGING VIEWS OF TEACHER WORK AND TEACHER LEARNING

Anne Shirley began her teaching career at the age of 16 in a one-room schoolhouse spanning multiple grade levels on Prince Edward Island in a school that she herself had graduated from only two years earlier. And even though her students triumphed on the annual examinations, Anne, after just two years, decided to go to college to study. "I'm really glad Anne is going to college," observed Ms. Bell. But Ms. Andrews did not agree: "I don't see that Anne needs any more education." Why would anyone need to go to college to learn anything useful for a career as a teacher?

(Montgomery, 1984, p. 428)

There have been remarkable changes in the landscape for teacher preparation since the time of Anne Shirley. The growth in understanding that teaching, including elementary teaching, is demanding intellectual work contributed significantly to the professionalization of teaching. The path toward the professionalization of teaching, however, is not fully realized. The professionalization of teaching is challenged by a widely held view that the work of teachers is technical in nature and that the preparation of teachers is largely a matter of training, not education.

The work of a professional is characterized by at least seven essential features. First, the work of a professional is tied to areas of significance in our lives. We use the term *professional* to describe the work of individuals who work in areas of law, medicine, the sciences, and education. Second, the disciplines that surround these professions have rich and deep knowledge bases that are constantly expanding through research and inquiry. Third, professions are situated within working spaces that are highly ambiguous and nuanced. Seldom is there a clear right or wrong way to respond to situations. Fourth, professions are characterized by highly contextualized decision-making that is responsive to the local context. Fifth, most of the professions are client-oriented. Professionals serve clients and are responsible to their clients more so than to the institutional contexts in which they work. Sixth, professions have extended layers of preparation in their field. Finally, and seventh, the learning of professionals continues throughout their lives and is tied to their practice. Professional practice is a space for growth.

Technicians are different from professionals in almost all of these seven areas. This is not to say that professionals don't acquire important technical skills. Nor is this to say that technicians are not important to society. Both technicians and professionals work hard and make important contributions. The point is simply that their work is different in ways that matter. Training is important in support of technicians and the development of technical knowledge. Education is important in the support of professionals and the development of practical knowledge. The supportive institutional contexts for technicians and professionals are different. Professionals need space for decision-making and reflection. Professionals benefit from dialogue with peers and mentors around practice. Technicians benefit from clear and explicit plans for how work is to be completed. Supervision and feedback are important in technical work.

To continue on the path toward the professionalization of teaching we must consider new understandings for how teachers learn and how teacher educators can support growth. We must examine some of the most widely held beliefs surrounding teaching and some of our most common traditions in teacher preparation that are limiting our potential as professionals. What are our goals? What is our practice? Through this chapter we strive to develop a consciousness of the present that is informed, in part, by an examination of the past. We strive to develop clarity on the challenges we face in making teaching more powerful for the future.

A Historical Perspective on Schooling in the United States

The schools and classrooms that we see in our neighborhoods today carry forward a lot of historical thinking around education and society. The spaces of hallways, classrooms, play areas, teacher's lounges, lunchrooms, gym areas, and principal's offices are as essential to today's schools as the schools of the early nineteenth century. The routines, the schedules, the movement of students and teachers are familiar and part of the norms for "doing school." Without textbooks, homework, curriculum guides, grouping and sorting of students, tests, grades, lectures, and the conferences with parents would you even have a school? "Crowds," "praise," and "power," as described by Philip Jackson (1990) in researching classroom life, are as recognizable today as they were a half a century ago. Why have schools been so resistant to change when everyone is calling for change?

History is powerful in shaping the present in ways that we might not always be conscious of. To unpack this history just a bit is useful as a starting place for a conversation around what are possibilities for change and what are the sources of resistance. Access to schools for all kids was a central tenet of the Common Schools Movement in the United States that began in the 1840s and continued through the early years of the twentieth century. Education was seen as essential to a democratic way of life. Public education should be universal, free, and compulsory. State supported public school systems became the goal across the country.

While the goal of education for all in the Common School Movement was a worthy one, the pressure on school systems to offer a quality education was tremendous as a function of the numbers of students entering schools. The massive waves of immigration during the late nineteenth and early twentieth century were testing the capacity of schools to serve. How can we offer schooling for all? And with that question, what kind of schooling can we offer for all? Did "all" mean for everyone? Does everyone include girls, non-citizens, and children of different races and religious beliefs? When does schooling stop being for everyone and for free? How do high schools, colleges, and universities fit into this plan? Is it acceptable that the schools serving wealthier communities, where local taxes are used to support schools, offer children more resources than the schools that serve lower income communities? These questions were addressed through political decisions made at the turn of the twentieth century based on social and economic considerations. The decisions that were made at this time have continued, for the most part, to shape schooling in the United States today.

The best hope for meeting the challenge of limited resources and growing numbers of students was found in the principles of scientific management. The "efficiency" movement was born out of the industrial revolution. Factory production of materials could be made more profitable by carefully minimizing the cost of input (materials, labor, time) and maximizing profit. The "stop watch" and efficiency analysis were key tools in the reform of production in the transition from the labor intensive work of craftsman in the past to the demands of the twentieth century. Of course, working conditions may not be optimal and wages might not be fair but that is just the reality of capitalism. The kinds of oppressive practices associated with the efficiency era gave birth to the labor union movement and the fights for workers' rights (as well as the first child labor laws).

If we can build a car efficiently we can certainly educate children efficiently following the same principles. Bobbitt wrote two books that spoke to these issues: *The Curriculum* (1918) and *How to Make a Curriculum* (1924). His theory of curriculum development was based on the same principles of scientific management described by Frederick Winslow Taylor's (1911) efforts to make industry more efficient. There must be a focus in curriculum development on creating measureable outcomes and organizing the system to minimize cost and maximize production.

Implicit in this efficiency model was an envisioned society where individuals assumed different roles and responsibilities. The belief was we should not be preparing everyone for the same job. That would be inefficient. Society demands both highly educated people (e.g., the doctors, lawyers, and scientists) as well as laborers prepared with the basic skills needed to build and serve. Schools must fulfill a social purpose and prepare individuals for a variety of roles based on their capabilities and interests. Schools should be organized with different tracks for different kinds of students based on their abilities. There should be academic as well as vocational programs (that are terminal). The "eugenics" movement, popular in this same time period, viewed intelligence as fixed and bound up in genetics and race. The more capable are just more capable and should be treated accordingly. The less capable are just less capable and should be treated accordingly. Everyone needs to be prepared to fit into their place in society.

The Technical Perspective on Teaching and Learning

How might schools be shaped toward an efficiency model? First, you frame schools as factories and the products they produce are citizens with requisite knowledge and skills. You set clear goals for knowledge production and make clear links between the outcomes and the experiences that maximize progress toward the goals. Divide the curriculum, following Bobbitt, into measureable outcomes. Emphasize models of teaching that are designed to deliver knowledge in efficient chunks Herbart's (1806) "object lesson" structure for teaching concepts and McMurry and McMurry's (1897) recitation lessons served this purpose well. Divide students according to ability. Track students and expect different things from different students that are aligned with their future role in society.

Hire teachers who can enact this system as any laborer might engage in factory work. Thus teaching (as an "occupation") and teachers, at the turn of the twentieth century were located closer to the labor force rather than the professional community. While Horace Mann (1865), in the creation of the "normal school" model for the preparation of common school teachers, was convincing that some form of advanced education was necessary for teachers, he believed a year or two of preparation beyond high school was more than sufficient. Mann believed teaching to be a behavior that could be described clearly in terms of basic skills and competencies. The skills and competencies could be trained and measured. You should not have to pay teachers much, rely on women who don't need as much income and are naturally good at the nurturing role. Don't require or expect them to make decisions. They don't need much preparation. Principals can manage the system and keep track of efficiency. Supervise carefully as a factory manager would.

The efficiency model for production aligned perfectly with the work of psychologists of the early twentieth century who focused on behaviorism as the guiding principle for teaching and learning. E. L. Thorndike is regarded by historians as the most influential psychologists of the first half of twentieth century. His works in the study of learning have shaped educational theories and practices even to the present. Thorndike was part of the Progressive education movement. He believed that the scientific study of learning could be used to guide the organization of schools, the structure of a curriculum, and the development of teaching practices. Thorndike (1913) believed that learning was governed by certain "laws" that were discoverable through scientific methods that rested on the careful measurement of outcomes.

Thorndike's first three laws (Smith, 2001) were stated as:

> **The law of effect.** Responses are selected and connected to situations or are disconnected from situations depending upon the consequences they produce. Responses that meet with a pleasurable response or consequence will tend to be strengthened and repeated. Responses that meet with an uncomfortable response or consequence will tend not to be strengthened nor repeated.
>
> **The law of exercise.** Repeated use strengthens a connection. Disuse will weaken it.
>
> **The law of readiness.** If physically ready the connection is satisfying for the organism. In addition to these three basic laws Thorndike formulated a number of subordinate laws developed. Taken together, these basic and subordinate laws became the basis for instructional design principles that emphasize the need for clearly defined behavioral outcomes, the Progressive movement from the simple to the complex in these targeted outcomes, the importance of practice (trial and error) and feedback, the effects of rewards and punishment as shaping learning.

Schools were never organized to provide any kind of deep learning—at least not the schools targeted toward the masses. Schools were designed to be efficient in producing capable citizens who could make a living and contribute to productivity. The schools we have today were built like any factory to be efficient in production of a product that has value to the economy. Teachers are assembly line workers tasked with doing their assigned tasks. Students are the outputs—the products that become commodities that feed neatly into an economic and social system. Economic and social stability are served by an educational system that nurtures conformity and competence. The accountability era, the attention to standards (as in the Common Core), and the emphasis on high stakes testing are simply extensions of the view of schooling that has been dominant for over a century in the United States.

The Practice Perspective

What if, instead of an efficiency model, we organized schools to maximize human potential? Schools might look very different from what we currently have in place. What if we built a curriculum for writing, as an example, around what writers do rather than around the essential skills that writers *need to know* in order to do what they do? What if we built a curriculum for science, as an example, around what scientists do rather than around the essential skills that scientists *need to know* in order to do what they do? What if we built a curriculum for art, as an example, around what artists do rather than around the essential skills that artists *need to know* in order to do what they do? How might this curriculum look different from an essentialist curriculum organized and perhaps "better" in the ways both students and a society are served? What if we regarded our teaching as directed toward opportunities rather than objectives?

This alternative conception of curriculum has been labeled, historically, as a curriculum that emphasizes "doing" and "experience." Most often this curriculum is articulated as "child centered" in that the curriculum is flexible and adapted to the interests and needs of the students. John Dewey was a leading advocate for such a curriculum. The movement met with some success in the 1920–1940 period as educational leaders, teachers, and parents pushed back on the dehumanization of schools in the efficacy period. But the pressure of efficiency and the hold of behaviorism on thinking about learning eventually won out and the movement became regarded as an historical blip in the movement toward accountability.

The cognitive revolution in psychology in the latter half of the twentieth century led us to think about teaching and learning in ways that challenge the dominant perspective. Thinking became the focus in learning, not behavior. The social practice movement of the twenty-first century is demanding that we go even further in our thinking about teaching and learning. Knowledge is not passed on from teachers to students. Knowledge is socially and culturally constructed in doing and experiencing and imbued with emotional response and situated in a context as well. Workshop models of teaching, project-based learning, inquiry curricula, problem-based learning, and service learning are all rooted in this general mindset.

Practice has become a key concept in this turn. Language practices are what we do with language in a variety of settings and for a variety of purposes. Lawyers practice law. Medical doctors and nurses practice medicine. Only in teaching do we describe practice not as what we do but as getting ready for what we do—more in the way an athlete prepares than in the doing of education. We don't want doctors practicing on us to get ready for their *real* patients any more than we want preservice teachers practicing to get ready for their *real* students. We want to reclaim the term *practice* as professional doing. When professionals practice, they are always growing in their craft. This is one of the things that makes the practice so powerful in a profession. We are not technicians executing a routine—although from the outside it may appear routine. We are professionals growing in our practice.

Practices exist within communities. Certain communities, for example, have ways of using language that may be different than other communities. There are norms within these communities for what, how, and when certain things are said (or unsaid). The community defines these. Participation in that community requires that the individual follow these rules. In some cases, these rules of practice may have been formalized and stated (as in spelling rules). Such moves toward standardization of practice are made for many different reasons, but more often the rules for practice are tacit and have to be learned within that community.

Lave and Wenger (1991) introduced the term "legitimate peripheral participation" in describing the processes by which someone enters into a community of practice. To illustrate this concept, let's take something like an informal book club as a community of practice. The newcomer to the book club may spend quite a bit of time on the outside of the circle listening and observing. There may be movements into participate but these may be a the very lowest levels of engagement. Gradually, the newcomer becomes more familiar and comfortable within the community and begins to participate more fully and more deeply. There may be rules to help the newcomer work their way in but these are more often than not expressed as ways to keep people out rather than facilitate entry. Far more important is the mentoring that goes on by the current members supporting, encouraging, and explaining the process of being fully participatory. It is a social, cultural, political, and intellectual process.

Rogoff (1995) described learning from this sociocultural perspective as operating on three planes—apprenticeship, guided participation, and participatory appropriation. She describes these three planes as inseparable and non-hierarchical. Apprenticeship involves active individuals participating with others in a culturally organized activity that has as part of its purpose the development of mature participation by the less experienced people. Guided participation refers to the processes and systems of involvement between people as they communicate and coordinate efforts while participating in a culturally valued activity. Participatory appropriation refers to how individuals change through their involvement in one or another activity in the process becoming prepared for subsequent involvement in related activities. This preparation path unfolds as a process of becoming, not as incremental skills acquisition. The practice turn is gaining momentum, internationally, as a result of the perceived failures of schools to achieve the goals of education through traditional forms of instruction and the belief that reform in teacher preparation is the most promising path to improving teaching (Zeichner, 2015). You might see in these theories implications for teaching and teacher education that are potentially transformative.

Reflection

John Dewey was a contemporary of Thorndike. The two men shared an association with the Progressive movement and a focus on scientific thinking—but in very different ways. Dewey's work was rooted more in educational philosophy than in educational psychology. Dewey was an advocate for pragmatism.

Reality, experience, and experimental inquiry were viewed as the test of worthiness of ideas. A pragmatic approach demanded a careful look at data (experience) and patterns that could be used to infer principles.

In one of his earliest works, *How We Think* (Dewey, 1910), Dewey proposed the development of scientific thinking (as a habit of the mind) as the goal of education. Dewey believed that " ... the native and unspoiled attitude of childhood, marked by ardent curiosity, fertile imagination, and love of experimental inquiry, is near, very near, to the attitude of the scientific mind" (Preface). Dewey focused the book on reflective thought that arises out of engagement with a problem or uncertainty. The person examines the situation carefully gathering data. "The data at hand cannot supply the solution; they can only suggest it" (p. 13). The person considers thoroughly the possible options and their consequences. The person takes action—and even then in a tentative way that a scientist might embark on an experiment.

Dewey (1910/1997) uses the metaphor of a fork in the road to characterize reflective thought. A person encounters an obstacle and must make a choice. Which path to follow? "Difficulty or obstruction in the way of reaching a belief brings us, however, to a pause. In the suspense of uncertainty, we metaphorically climb a tree; we try to find some standpoint from which we may survey additional facts and, getting a more commanding view of the situation, may decide how the facts stand related to one another" (Dewey, 1910/1997, p. 11). Dewey grounds his representation of thought in uncertainty and experimentation. "Demand for the solution of a perplexity is the steadying and guiding factor in the entire process of reflection" (Dewey, 1910/1997, p. 12). Dewey also makes the important point here that reflective thought is not just cerebral but imbedded in activity. Reflective thought is knowing and doing.

Dewey's notions around thinking and reflection are important in our thinking about learning through practice. Reflection is both short-term problem-solving (the fork in the road) that must be addressed in the moment and long-term sense-making around planning for the future and making sense of experience toward principled practice. Schön (1983) asserts that this quality of reflection is one of the essential features of professional life. He uses the terms *reflection in-practice* and *reflection on-practice* to describe the importance of reflection in learning.

> **Reflection in-practice.** These are the decisions and the processes we use to make adjustments in what we are doing in the moment based on context and expectation.
> **Reflection on-practice.** These are the decisions we make about moving forward stepping out of a professional experience. These are decisions that relate to next steps and also reflections around our own growth.

The reflective practitioner takes time to ponder these processes as a source of guidance for the future.

The Practice of Teacher Education

The technical view of teacher education is best represented in the Competency Based Teacher Education (CBTE) movement of the 1960s. As a first step, the functions of teaching and the behaviors of teaching are clearly described and arrayed from simple to complex. These skills are introduced and practiced (in the sense of repeated) to achieve efficient and accurate demonstration of the behavior). These skills are introduced and modeled in courses or modules of study. There is a careful progression of skills introduced and careful monitoring of control. Eventually, the skills are applied in the context of teaching in classrooms (a "practicum" experience).

In considering what professionals know and how they learn, we are drawn to a different model from the competency or skills mastery view espoused by behaviorists. We believe that teachers rely on what Shulman (1986) has termed "pedagogical content knowledge" (PCK) in shaping their practices. In turn, their practice experiences inform and reshape their pedagogical knowledge. How this knowledge is represented and enacted is complicated. We have come to believe that this kind of knowledge is revealed in the activity structures that teachers use in their classrooms to enact the curriculum. In our work around teaching practices we have found the Concerns Based Adoption Model (CBAM) to be helpful. The CBAM model is considerate of both the concerns and actions of teachers as they engage in change. The CBAM model also introduced the concept of innovation configuration as a useful tool in monitoring the change process, outlining the core and optional components of implementation of a program (Hall and Loucks, 1977). The innovation configuration describes specifically the changes that are required on the part of the individual adopting the change.

The practice view, a professional alternative, for teacher education is represented in the conception offered by Grossman and McDonald (2008). They describe the responsibility of teacher educators to engage new teachers in:

> **Demonstrations.** This involves focusing in on practices and observing them and engaging with them deeply. These demonstrations might be offered through video or simulations or they may actually involve the focused observation of a teacher in practice.
>
> **Deconstructions.** This involves looking carefully at the models and pulling them apart to examine the essential features of the practice. Where is there variability? Where is there consistency? What are the guiding principles driving the practice? What are the forms of adaptations that are made?
>
> **Approximations.** This involves "trying out" and "trying on" new practices. These experiences may be carefully structured (e.g, tutoring) or more open ended (e.g, in a regular teaching experience).

Teaching practices are the focus for preparation. There is no sequencing of isolated skills or a lock-step progression of skills but an emphasis on moving the new teacher into practices. Teaching is a community of practice that new teachers must step into through participation. This is not a throw them in, sink or swim approach. This is carefully orchestrated to insure success and growth. There is explicit teaching and explanation where conversations and problem solving are keys to success.

We have taken the notion of innovation configurations and adapted it for our use in our work around coaching and mentoring. As we will address in Chapter 5, we use the term Activity Configurations instead of innovation configurations to emphasize that we are focusing not on the adoption of a program but on an instructional activity structure that lives within a setting with goals, practices, participants, norms, and occurring within a community. This pedagogical content knowledge forms a vital part of the coaching and mentoring support that we offer to preservice teachers.

The Critical Turn: Oppressive and Liberatory Alternatives

We are going to expect the (nearly) impossible for your work in mentoring and coaching. We are going to challenge you to enact a practice-based, professional view of teacher learning in spaces dominated by the technical view. By taking on the challenges to mentor and coach in this way, you will be preparing new teachers for the real challenges they will face as teachers striving to be professional in this same technical world. These are as much political stances as they are pedagogical.

We typically organize schools around little pieces of knowledge and skills that are intended to build up students' "capital." The teacher's role is transmission of this knowledge and skills. We are building a product (not unlike manufacturing a car) that is added to with efficiency and know outcomes and standards. We (teachers) give students the problems to solve, the questions they need to answer, and the acceptable versions of the answers. Freire (1970) critiques this model for being dehumanizing in that it never engages the learner as a person who brings experience, perspective, and a purpose to education. The banking model, according to Freire, has done a remarkable job of seeing to it that schools replicate the inequities that exist in our society.

As described in the previous chapter, Freire (1970/1995) argues that a problem-posing curriculum that focuses on learners posing the problems they will address is the more powerful and more humane alternative. The teacher's role is in constructing the curriculum that reflects content that is important to the learner. Freire's writing is often characterized as radical and revolutionary. These labels are thrown on Freire's work in an attempt to dismiss his position. Some people are nervous about the identification of opportunities offered to students who come from positions of privilege and the absence of these opportunities to those who are on the margins of society.

We are basing our view on the principle of educating (serving) children in ways that empower them and help them become more fully human. We ask that any teaching involves a reflection of what is being taught and how something is being taught with the question of: Is this in the best interest of each and every student? If the answer to that question is yes, then you are on the path of becoming a powerful teacher. If the answer is no, then you have the responsibility to adapt the curriculum and the teaching in ways that your students deserve. This is radical, but at the core of the social contract we have as professionals.

This version of teaching not always easy and requires, what Cochran-Smith (1991) describes as "against the grain" teaching. The system assesses a student and labels him a "poor" reader (or whatever other label divides kids by ability/skill). How do you deal with this in your teaching? Do you resist? How? This may not feel obvious to you as something that affects identity in negative ways, but you might want to explore the effects more deeply and the need and the alternatives. This process is what Freire refers to as conscientization ... we are building our awareness of the features of our work and questioning those. It is a process and a stance that leads to, what Freire describes, as a liberating pedagogy.

Where to Start?

Words Matter

Our practice is filled with language (words, phrases) that are a legacy of our past commitment to behaviorism and efficiency. We describe our teaching as "lessons" when so much of the teaching that we do may be more interactive and student led. We describe our objectives are predetermined and imposed rather than as something we help our students formulate. We refer to our teaching as driven by objectives rather than opportunities. We talk of management as essential when we could be talking about building learning communities. Thinking about these words and historical meanings that they bring forward is one place to begin to build a different kind of classroom—not new words on top of the same expectations. What we want is new ways with words, to borrow Shirley Brice Heath's (1983) term, that reflect what we envision for the classroom. We draw on Johnston's (2004) idea of *Choice Words*: specific naming and appreciation of learning, growth, and cooperation.

Dichotomies Can Be Dangerous

After spending an entire chapter distinguishing between a technical and professional perspective on teaching and teacher education, it may come as a surprise for us to warn you on the dangers of dichotomous thinking. But we will. There is something in our nature that likes to divide, categorize, and name things. While this work can help us concentrate and focus, it can also lead us to see dichotomies as real. Consider the division of assessment and teaching. Two different things? But in the most authentic teaching we do we are always assessing and in the most authentic assessments we do we are always teaching. Teachers and learners are totally different right? But, when is a teacher not learning? And when is a learner not teaching? Cognitive, affective, and perceptual outcomes are different. Right? But what about the literature on embodied learning that suggests growth is more powerful in contexts where the physical, the emotional, and the cognitive are all engaged at the same time? Have you ever considered the differences you get when you ask yourself the question, "What did you learn through this experience?" as compared to "How did you grow through this experience?" A simple shifting of words like this can reveal a great deal about how our words and word choices can limit our work potential.

Division can assist our thinking and conversation but it can also sell short on the opportunities to grow. Adopting a practice perspective toward teaching and teacher education does not mean total rejection of the technical. The practice perspective is a context for considering the technical and procedural parts of learning. This is the kind of thinking that makes mini-lessons so powerful in the context of workshop or experiential learning. These direct, explicit moments in teaching are powerful tools.

A Case: Balancing Technical and Professional

In our second year of developing CARE, we worked with a cooperating teacher and a graduate student, Abigail. At the time, she was in her fifth year of teaching fourth grade at this campus, and she had experienced many changes on her team over the years. Abigail described herself as a "laid-back" person, who liked to "go with the flow." During this year, we paired Abigail with Kourtney, a preservice teacher from our literacy cohort, who had returned to the university to earn her teaching certification as a post-baccalaureate. Abigail and Kourtney worked on a campus that was certified as an International Baccalaureate school, and Abigail was pleased to work in this context because she understood that "we [teachers] are expected to implement a workshop model rather than a product based model in reading and writing" [Interview 1, August 2013]. Abigail and Kourtney were the same age, and Kourtney had two years of experience teaching in a private school on the west coast. They were fast friends and colleagues; however, they did, at the same time, have to work through the tensions of having different answers to the question, "Is this in the best interest of each and every student?"

Abigail and Kourtney appreciated and valued their students' knowledge, and they positioned their students as collaborators—drawing from Freire's (1970) notion on the importance of co-construction of knowledge between teacher and student. For Abigail, the focus of her instruction was content and ensuring that the curriculum requirements were being met systematically. For Kourtney, the focus of her instruction was on "teaching against the grain" by pursuing a critical literacy approach across content areas. Abigail and Kourtney respected each other's approach to teaching; yet, in their relationship as mentor and mentee, they did compromise, make space, and support each other with the other's focus.

As a fourth grade teacher, Abigail felt a strong obligation to her students and school that her class was prepared for the state exams in writing, reading, and math. On the other hand, she felt a strong obligation to her students, Kourtney, and herself to teach in the most authentic and meaningful ways. Before Kourtney began her student teaching semester, where she would be teaching alongside Abigail each day (and slowly taking over the lead), Abigail expressed her tension in a meeting with us,

> Then I think, too, I'm worried—I hate cramming for tests and I try really hard to bring in little pieces along the way, so I don't feel like we are cramming. But I don't want her [Kourtney] to see what cramming looks like. At some point it'll probably... We have a lot of struggling students in this classroom. Making sure they are all where they need to be—I'm concerned about these things. On the one hand, I don't mind trying new things [e.g., critical literacy]. But, then knowing that *my* name is on the contract. It's gonna be *my* name that goes on for interviews [e.g., future positions]. That's scary to me. I don't think she [Kourtney] would mess it up at all. But, not having my hands on it the way I would normally because I'm trying to give her those experiences scares me. [Interview 2, December 2013]

As teacher educators, we are always grateful for the honesty and vulnerability that the cooperating teachers and preservice teachers bring with them as they engage in this process of becoming teachers and teacher educators themselves. We know, based on our conversations with many cooperating teachers, that the tensions that Abigail expresses in this conversation are familiar for many inservice teachers, whose students are required to take multiple standardized exams at the end of each school year. The pressure of testing does not only affect the students in negative ways, but as we can see with the case of Abigail and Kourtney, these tests affect the well-being of our teachers and influence their approach to teaching, coaching, and mentoring. Abigail shared, "What's hard for me is that I felt like more and more the people who are oppressed in the education system are the teachers. That's who's oppressed in the education system. That has been something I am still mulling over and that bothers me" [Interview 2, December 2013]. We fully recognize the pressures felt by Abigail are real and hard, and we hope that with CARE, colleagues are able to address these tensions head-on through problem-posing dialogue. Abigail knew that there were many parts of the day, semester, and year, where she and Kourtney would just "shut my door" and teach their students in the way they thought they "needed to teach."

This case study is intended to illuminate the ongoing development of teaching as a profession. Although, we want to understand that teaching is moving away from being a technical endeavor, the existence of the standardized tests and the intense pressures felt by classroom teachers and the school administrators to pass these tests as a testimony to quality of the education stands in stark contrast to the development of teaching as a professional endeavor, where we advocate for community and the cognitive, social, and emotional well-being of all involved.

Some Thinking and Talking To Do

- *Anne of Avonlea* is a classic piece of literature. It is not a book on how to teach but in contextualizing Anne's life in at the turn of the twentieth century we have a rich glimpse in the life of a teacher. What other teacher stories, historically situated, might provide for rich discussion and reflection on the changes in the teaching profession?
- There were strong outcries against the application of the efficiency movement applied to education for the dehumanization of teaching. How might these concerns be relevant today?
- It's hard to argue against "efficiency." Why would we want to have inefficient schools? How do you frame a conversation around the pitfalls of efficiency driving our thinking about education and build a convincing argument for rethinking schools?
- Think of some practice you learned through legitimate peripheral participation (outside of education). What was that experience like for you? How were mentors active in supporting you into the practice?
- Changing the words we use is difficult. How can you have a conversation around education without using words like lesson, goals, outcomes, accountability, and skills? How could the conversations be made more powerful through the introduction of new words?
- We offered an historical perspective on teachers as technicians and schooling as oriented toward essentialist and atomistic models of curriculum. Why does this perspective continue to dominate despite advances in thinking around learning?
- Freire really challenges us to think about power and oppression in schooling. Are these real challenges that we need to be aware of and prepared to face in our work with new teachers? What if you don't want to be a radical and challenge the existing system, can you still coach and mentor?
- What does "against the grain" teaching (or by extrapolation, "against the grain" coaching), mean to you?

References

Bobbitt, J. F. (1918). *The curriculum*. Boston, MA: Houghton Mifflin Company.

Bobbitt, J. F. (1924). *How to make a curriculum*. Boston, MA: Houghton Mifflin Company.

Cochran-Smith, M. (1991). Learning to teach against the grain. *Harvard Educational Review, 61*(3), 279–311.

Dewey, J. (1910). *How we think*. Boston, MA: D. C. Heath and Co.

Freire, P. (1970). *Pedagogy of the oppressed*. (M. B. Ramos, Trans.). New York, NY: Bloomsbury. (Original work published in 1968).

Grossman, P. and McDonald, M. (2008). Back to the future: Directions for research in teaching and teacher education. *American Educational Research Journal, 45*(1), 184–205.

Hall, G. E. and Loucks, S. F. (1977). A developmental model for determining whether the treatment is actually implemented. *American Educational Research Journal, 14*(3), 263–276.

Heath, S. B. (1983). *Ways with words: Language, life and work in communities and classrooms*. Cambridge, MA: Cambridge university Press.

Jackson, P. W. (1990). *Life in classrooms*. New York, NY: Teachers College Press.

Johnston, P. H. (2004). *Choice words: How our language affects children's learning*. New York: Stenhouse Publishers.

Lave, J. and Wenger, E. (1991). *Situated learning: Legitimate peripheral participation*. Cambridge, UK: Cambridge University Press.

Mann, H. (1865). *Life and works of Horace Mann*. (Vol. 1). Boston, MA: Walker, Fuller, and Company.

McMurry, C. A. and McMurry, F. M. (1897). *The method of the recitation*. Bloomington, IL: Public School Publishing Company.

Montgomery, L. M. (1984). *Anne of Avonlea*. New York: Bantam Books.

Rogoff, B. (1995). Observing sociocultural activity on three planes: participatory appropriation, guided participation, and apprenticeship. In J. V. Wertsch, P. D. Rio, and A. Alvarez (Eds.), *Sociocultural studies of mind* (pp. 252). Cambridge UK: Cambridge University Press.

Schön, D. A. (1983). *The reflective practitioner: How professionals think in action*. New York, NY: Basic Books.

Shulman, L. S. (1986). Those who understand: Knowledge growth in teaching. *Educational Researcher, 15*(2), 4–14.

Smith, W. A. (2001). *E. L. Thorndike. Twentieth Century Thinkers in Adult and Continuing Education* (pp. 77). London: Kogan Page.

Taylor, F. W. (1911). *The principles of scientific management*. New York, NY: Harper and Brothers.

Thorndike, E. L. (1913). *The psychology of learning* (Vol. 2). Teachers College, Columbia University.

Zeichner, K. (2015). The politics of learning to teach from experience. In V. Ellis and J. Orchard (Eds.) *Learning teaching from experience: Multiple perspectives and international contexts* (pp. 257–267). London: Bloomsbury Academic.

PART II

The Coaching with CARE Model and Cycle

4

THE COACHING WITH CARE MODEL

Ubuntu … speaks of the very essence of being human. You share what you have. It is to say, "My humanity is caught up, is inextricably bound up, in yours." We belong in a bundle of life. We say, "A person is a person through other persons." A person with ubuntu is open and available to others, affirming of others, does not feel threatened that others are able and good, for he or she has a proper self-assurance that comes from knowing that he or she belongs in a greater whole and is diminished when others are humiliated or diminished, when others are tortured or oppressed, or treated as if they were less than who they are.

(Desmond Tutu)

In this chapter we present an overview of the Coaching with CARE model. In the chapters that follow we will explore the components of the model in greater depth. Embedded in the model, you will find many of the key concepts and perspectives introduced in the earlier chapters. The model has been developed through our research with teachers in our teacher education program. It is unfinished and evolving. This unfinished quality is important to consider as we work with the various elements. We begin with a discussion of the overarching perspective and then move to consider each of the components.

The Perspective of CARE

CARE is both a theme and an acronym for the major components of the model. We view mentoring and coaching as relational acts that have strong moral and ethical elements. We have a responsibility to help grow teachers who will become powerful in their work with children. We have a responsibility to the children they will teach in the moment and through their careers. We adopt CARE as the central theme for our relational work and moral responsibilities.

You will have decisions to make as a coach and mentor that will challenge you. What are the principles that will guide you in this decision-making? You could be rule-bound. Follow the steps, procedures, and standards established within your institution as a guide and when in doubt, ask an authority to tell you what to do. You could follow a set of least work, least trouble, and least risk principles to guide you. "Let's just get through this without any problems." Neither of these two approaches to decision-making will work for your goal of supporting powerful teaching and teacher learning. The most difficult decisions you will face do not have yes/no or right/wrong paths to follow. In the first case, no handbook, no authority is going to know the contexts and relationships you are negotiating in ways that can prescribe your decisions. In the second case, seeking the path of least resistance will not prepare a teacher for the challenges they will face in their teaching lives.

Care has been widely considered as a guiding principle for decision-making in complex situations. Ubuntu, as described in the opening of this chapter by Desmond Tutu (2000), is based on the principle of care. Ubuntu is found widely in African cultures as a principle of community and responsibility. It is both a personal quality and a collective quality of a culture. The word used to describe this philosophy takes on different names in different African languages (the term Ubuntu is Zulu in its origins). We are all connected. If one fails or falls short in reaching their goals, then we have all failed and fallen short. We succeed when we all succeed. In the South African national educational policy, Ubuntu is a mandated consideration for all lessons that are taught in schools. How does the lesson build a sense of Ubuntu in the classroom learning community or how does a lesson put this principle at risk? If the new teachers we work with fall short of their goals, we have all failed. We succeed when we all succeed.

Care has also been explored in the moral development literature. Perhaps the most striking example of care is found in the work of Carol Gilligan (1996). She conducted research looking at the ways in which individuals approached difficult moral dilemmas. Her work was critical of traditional approaches to moral decision-making that relied on sets of guiding principles that one follows in doing the "right" thing. Gilligan focused her research on women in particular and found that decision-making around difficult moral dilemmas. She found a pattern among women that she identified as the caring principle. I should do what is the most caring thing to do in that moment and in that context. The caring thing to do may not be what the person who is in need wants—or it may be. The caring thing is not the "right" thing to do as much as it is what can and should be done in the moment and moving forward. Today, the caring principle is often used across professional domains (e.g., medical care) as an ethical principle.

Nel Noddings has done extensive writing around the principle of care in education. Her first major work explored a feminist perspective on ethical and moral decision-making in education. A caring person "is one who fairly regularly establishes caring relations and, when appropriate maintains them over time."

She asks, "what are we like" when we engage in caring encounters? "Perhaps the first thing we discover about ourselves," she continues, "is that we are receptive; we are attentive in a special way" (Noddings, 2002, p. 13).

Noddings (2002) distinguishes between "caring for" and "caring about." Caring for is represented and enacted in caring encounters. Caring about is a more general stance around social justice and broader social meanings that enables the individual to engage in caring for. Noddings sees the infusion of the caring perspective in education as a means for cultivating our broader society toward an ethic of care (along the direction of Ubuntu). There will be many times during your mentoring experience when you will struggle with fork-in-the-road decisions that don't seem to have a right or wrong choice. "What is the caring thing to do?" is the question that will guide you.

The Components of the CARE Model

The letters in the word CARE speak to some of the essential elements in the model. We have found that it works better if we proceed backwards in order as a path of description and initial exploration (E-R-A-C, instead of C-A-R-E). In the sections that follow, we begin conversations that we will continue throughout the book. We believe that appropriating the model of CARE includes both engaging in procedures for coaching and developing practices that align theoretically with the dimensions of CARE, as we describe below.

Experience

The CARE model is committed to experiential learning. Doing is a powerful form of learning. The embodied work of teaching cannot be divided neatly into categories isolated from one another. As with most experiential learning, you have high levels of motivation as teaching is a career choice. There is compelling evidence from research into teacher learning that the practicum experiences are the most powerful in shaping learning. As described earlier, the experiences you will offer are not the first for your preservice teacher. They have had years of experience, a lot of these experiences may have been less than positive, and one of your greatest challenges is to help them see teaching in terms of possibilities.

We can think of service learning experiences as a model. Within service learning there is a notion of "working with" and "working for." A service learning experience, for example, for Habitat for Humanity is around serving the people the house is being built for and working with a variety of people with different skill sets who come committed to the same vision. In the muddied world of education and accountability, we lose sight at times of whom we serve and who we serve with. We serve children and their parents. We serve with many different people who share expertise and responsibility for enabling young children to become powerful.

"Experience is the best teacher" is an old adage and one that still carries a lot of truth. Dewey contrasts experiences with educative experiences. Not all experiences are educative in the sense that they are contexts for growth. Educative experiences both challenge and connect (backward and forward). As we consider the kinds of experiences that are most powerful for preservice teachers we want to think about the progression of experiences that form a path of learning. Challenge is one of the more complicated and difficult areas to negotiate in supporting a novice. Following Vygotsky's (1978) conception of the zone of proximal development, we do not want the challenges in teaching experiences to overwhelm or frustrate nor do we want the work to be so easy that they simply replicate the known. We want the just-right challenges that will require the preservice teacher to grow with the scaffolding we can provide as mentors and coaches. Thinking forward just a bit around this notion of challenges is the notion that the preservice teacher should be creating challenging contexts for their students as well. Challenge, as Dewey (1938) reminds us, is at the heart of all learning.

What *challenged* you today to grow as a teacher?

What *challenged* our students to grow?

Reflection

The experience of challenge prompts consciousness of the strategies one is using to solve problems. A drive to work may be uneventful or it may be filled with challenges. When those challenges appear we become conscious of the mechanics and strategies around our effort. We can leave these in the moment, and fall short on the educative value of the experience, or we can reflect and strategize (e.g., leave earlier, take a different route). Teaching experiences are no different. Reflection is the primary tool for learning. We have already described two kinds of reflection around experience, following Schön; here we expand on these notions.

> **Reflection in action.** This kind of reflection centers on the changes or adaptations made in the moment. These are often the most difficult moments to capture and discuss, because they occur in the flow of practice. Often, we reflect in action because something isn't quite right—we find a flaw in our plans because of how the students respond. We make changes "in flight" to make things better. We don't always know that reflection in action has occurred unless we have a framework for describing our plans and our adaptations. Often, the coach's role is to observe and bring to the surface moments like these as rich spaces for deliberation.
>
> **Reflection on action.** We most commonly use this type of reflective practice when we talk, write, or think back on a lesson or activity and make sense of that experience. This is not a "should of" or "could of" analysis of regret but an earnest effort to identify areas or strategies we want to take forward into our teaching.

Sadly, reflection has become overused to the point in education, and especially, in teacher education, that it carries little meaning. We ask students to reflect on an article in the sense of thinking about it. We ask students to reflect on a video they observed in the sense of thinking about it. We are asking preservice teachers to reflect toward action. Guiding the novice through these kinds of experiences and learning to use reflection as a tool for learning is your primary focus as a coach.

In our work with the CARE model we have expanded reflection to include:

Reflecting into practice. This is the time just before teaching (literally the moments before teaching) when a teacher envisions the teaching that is to unfold.

Reflecting in practice. This is the reflection around changes and adaptations that are made inside of teaching.

Reflecting on practice. This is the time for looking at the potential growth points as a focus for the work of teacher learning.

Reflecting for practice. This is the reflecting we do in our planning for teaching.

Reflecting around practice. This is the kind of reflecting we do around practice that isn't specific to a moment in time and is outside of the coaching cycle we will describe in the next chapter.

As we move forward in explicating the CARE model we will elaborate on the coaching strategies that can support these various types of reflection.

Appreciative (Stances)

Education, in our view, is mired in deficit talk and deficit thinking. We talk about student needs in terms of what they don't know or can't do. We talk less about what the student wants to learn. We organize our curriculum around the essentialist model that keeps adding parts to the learner and being sure that we don't move forward without mastery. The extreme analysis of test performance—used to determine what students are not doing and focused on adapting instruction to those data—is a prime example of deficit thinking. The extreme versions of learning disability and the labels we place on kids who we regard as outside of the normal is replete with deficit thinking. The common view of coaching is similar. The coach's job is to fill in the holes in what a teacher needs to know and be able to do. Our analytic lens is always focused on the gaps. We fix kids; we fix teachers. We diagnose the problems and we prescribe the treatment, all with reference to the "normal" imbedded in the curriculum.

There is an alternative. We can focus our teaching on strength. We can focus our assessments on an appreciation for what the student (or preservice teacher) is doing and attempting to do. We can build scaffolds from the known to the new (the true sense of scaffolding) instead of scaffolding as filling in holes. We can use an asset based lens (What do they know and how can we use it?) rather than a deficit lens by looking at the resources learners draw on that we may not assume as relevant or important. We can follow the learner's lead in building a curriculum for them.

There is a principle in community development work that illustrates this contrast between deficit and appreciative perspectives and the power of the latter. An outsider (or a team of outsiders) could enter into a community and identify all the things that might be "wrong" from their expert perspective. The sanitation is poor. The infrastructure is lacking. The safety and security issues are high. All kinds of lists for action and strategic plans for prioritizing change could be made. This would be the deficit view. Another approach would be to engage with the community around their perceived needs and priorities for change. What do they want to see happen moving forward? Perhaps they want a playground or a sports field. A plan for action could be developed with the community following this plan. This would be appreciative or asset-based planning. Following the appreciative model, the capacity of the community to address issues is strengthened. Issues in the community that were not prioritized before will come into focus as their capacity grows.

As we engage with preservice teachers we might see a thousand different practices they can't do and need to learn. We might even begin to prioritize these in some way based on what we know about teaching. We are going to ask that you shift this focus to what you see the novice doing and thinking that has power and potential. How can we build on those noticingss? It's not that we are going to ignore all those things we noted in our engagement but we are going to trust the process that we will get to those things and much more through an asset lens. We are asking that you see the glass as "half full" and work from there. Pay attention to differences between the discourse of appreciation with the discourse of praise. They are different. Praise is power and authority used to direct. Appreciation happens as noticing and naming and extending. "I noticed that you .... Tell me more." "In teaching we sometimes call this ...." "What are some ways that we could extend this to be even more powerful for you moving forward?"

"C" Times Three

In our early explorations of the CARE model the C had just one word associated with it. As a result of our work, however, we have come to focus on three C's: Community, Critical, and Content.

Community

Consider all the different (and overlapping) communities that surround coaching and mentoring. There is the community of the two of you and the students in the classroom. There is the community of the school that you work in, as well as the parents and families that the school serves. There is your community with the preservice teacher. For the preservice teachers, there is also the community of those connected to the preservice teacher (e.g., a university supervisor, course instructors, program directors, and preservice teacher's peers in the preparation program). We will return to this community in Chapter 10, which is focused on collaborative coaching. And, finally, there is the community of those learning to coach and mentor. We think about these communities as more than contexts. We think of these communities as resources and processes that we can draw on as resources in our work.

The first community you'll attend to in your work with your preservice teacher is the classroom community. We will talk about establishing a sense in the classroom of "our" space, "our" students, and the work "we" do together. Next, you will begin to work on the community inside of your classroom, the ways that work is organized and the teacher's role within that classroom. Classroom management is a space where preservice teachers and novices often experience some of their greatest struggles. In part, at least at the preservice level, these needs are associated with the perception of no authority. "I'm not the real teacher in the classroom and the students won't do what I want them to do. How can I ever get control without being the teacher?" Authority, in traditional terms, is the key to a working classroom. Philip Jackson (1968/1990) framed this perspective on the classrooms around issues of "crowds, praise, and power." Speaking of the hidden curriculum of schooling, he argued that schools are crowded places in which order is created and maintained through praise of good behavior and control of that which is less preferred, and that being in classrooms depends on one's acceptance and compliance with the difference in authority between teacher and student. We know these concerns are real and that the authority perspective is dominant in the discourse of teaching, but we are going to work with you in this first part of the chapter to problem pose in a different way than is traditional with your preservice teacher around the classroom community.

The second layer of community we want to illuminate is the community of coaches that you might be working with. Based on the setting of your school and the context you work within, you may experience tensions in the appropriation of the CARE model (Hoffman et al., 2014). We are particularly attuned to the power of the community that is learning together strategies for coaching and mentoring. The interactions within this community are essential to learning. In the context of this community you will find support and challenge. As we move forward in this book, you will see specific suggestions for some ways to engage within this learning community. Moving forward, you will find that the conversations around practice that take place within this group will shape your learning more than anything else you experience beyond the experience of mentoring and coaching itself. This community will support your reflection and because there are many different mentors and many different novices you will see the need for flexibility in thinking forward. We will return to this notion of a coaching community in Chapter 12.

Critical

This is the actual C that existed within the original CARE model. We consider the term critical as a stance in multiple ways. There is the critical stance around social justice that we observe. We want to be conscious in our teaching about the ways in which our actions and thinking might limit or extend opportunities for historically marginalized groups such as minorities and women. In a sense, this is a call for Ubuntu in all our teaching work. We must be conscious in all of our teaching that we are affording opportunity and the highest of expectations for all to succeed.

There is also the sense of critical, not unrelated to the first, where we are attentive to the ways in which power and authority might be limiting our teaching potential. Are there mandates, restrictions, norms for practice that divert us from the kind of teaching to our students' needs? How can we examine and work around these forces to be the teacher our students need in the moment? We look more closely at the "critical" in coaching in Chapter 8.

Content

We are all experienced classroom teachers who worked across the elementary curriculum. As we have continued to work in mentoring and coaching across the curriculum we have come to recognize how our knowledge of the language arts informs our coaching in ways that we cannot draw on for areas like mathematics or science. We understand that there are some things about teaching and mentoring and coaching that apply broadly. However, we also know that disciplinary knowledge is important. Coaching might vary across academic disciplines and instructional approaches. In the previous chapter we pointed to the importance of pedagogical content knowledge for teaching. We view it as extremely important that coaches and mentors have access to the pedagogical content knowledge that teachers are drawing on in practice. We will address this topic more deeply in our discussions of Activity Configurations and later, in Chapter 9, in a more extensive treatment of disciplinary knowledge and support for teachers.

A Case: A Beginning Mentor

Louise is a teacher in a fourth grade classroom who was in our first cohort of master's students. Louise has taught in "self-contained"—classrooms, departmentalized classrooms, and what we call "self-contained," or classrooms in which she taught all subjects. She has always had students with special needs in her classroom, and has worked to build "a really caring and supportive community … getting the kids to really rely on each other more so than on the teacher." In her first years of teaching she was mentored by her peers and her principal who defined mentoring as checking that a person has planned effectively. Much of her prior experience with coaches included interactions that were "scary and threatening." In response, she strives to be a teacher and a mentor that values students' questions and inquiries, and to share her excitement for learning. Her community at the elementary school supported her orientation to her teaching, and her peers and community at the university became a touchstone for her changing orientation to mentoring.

Louise appropriated the CARE model in her first two years of working with our mentoring program. There were several ways that Louise showed her student teachers care through the model. First, Louise stayed true to herself. She trusted herself to tell her student teachers when she had an authentic wondering or feeling about a lesson or a student's participation in the classroom. However, she always balanced this commitment with prioritizing the student teacher: "My goal is always to let her think it through first ... or we think it through together first, but I don't want my statements to be clouding her process." Finally, she always appreciated and closed each conference with a positive: "I want to come back to, I noticed this, I really liked ...." "The kids were really engaged during this part and that was great."

It was not always easy for Louise to enact the CARE model, and she attributed her challenges to her own apprenticeship of observation, having been mentored in more directive ways. Louise called her work, "Quieting the voices in my head." She found coaching different from working with children, where she felt confident that she was responsive and valuing of their perspectives: "something switches when it's an adult and I want to tell them what to do." For Louise, this tension may exist because she has traditionally seen children as the learners and teachers as the experts. Often in the role of teacher, we believe that we need to know everything in order to be the best teacher for our students. She had to work to apply the principles of caring she had for her students to her student teacher, and this required a shift in thinking about her role. As Louise began to develop her own tools of mentoring and coaching, she was more apt to recognize herself as a teacher educator.

Louise found balance through the CARE model and was able to honor her own strengths as a mentor and temper her directive tendencies with more caring and reflective practices.

> My current philosophy is that I want to assist my student teacher in becoming reflective on her own practice by having conversations with her about what she noticed and why things went that way, and what she can take away from that for next time. At the same time, I also want to be able to share with her things that I have learned that have worked. So I guess that's the more directive part, and then letting her reflect and then helping her reflect is the more cognitive part, in my mind. That has changed from in the past, when I've wanted to be more directive and had student teachers do it my way.

With CARE, Louise was able to reflect into her own practice, and she realized that "my way" may be many different ways depending on the teacher. Louise could share her way as one way to support the preservice teacher's own way.

Some Thinking and Talking To Do

- Consider this scenario: We have a student teacher whom, despite all our efforts, is not being successful with the students in her class. It has come to the point that her limitations are affecting the students' learning and growth in negative ways. What's the caring thing to do?
- Is Ubuntu a metaphor that you would subscribe to as an ideal? How could a classroom encourage this perspective?
- Who is in the community supporting your development as a mentor and a coach? How is this community supporting you? How can you take greater advantage of them as a resource?
- How do you feel prepared to coach and mentor across disciplinary areas in the curriculum? Is it important? What might you need to work on and how?
- What experience in teaching have you had recently that you would describe as "educative"? What made this experience educative for you?
- "Needs" seems to have multiple meanings in education around the "deficit" and "appreciative" perspectives. What do you need as a mentor and coach? What are your strengths as a mentor and coach and how do your perceived needs flow from those strengths?

References

Dewey, J. (1938). *Experience and education*. New York, NY: Macmillan Press.

Gilligan, C. and Attanucci, J. (1996). The moral principle of care. In P. Banyard and A. Grayson (Eds.), *Introducing psychological research* (pp. 240–245). London, UK: Macmillan Education.

Hoffman, J. V., Mosley Wetzel, M., Maloch, B., Taylor, L., Adonyi Pruitt, A., Greeter, E., and Khan Vlach, S. (2014). Cooperating teachers coaching preservice teachers around literacy practices: A design/development study of Coaching with CARE. *63rd Yearbook of the Literacy Research Association*.

Jackson, P. W. (1968/1990). *Life in classrooms*. New York: Holt, Rinehart and Winston.

Noddings, N. (2002). *Educating moral people: A caring alternative to character education*. New York, NY: Teachers College Press.

Tutu, D. (2000). *No future without forgiveness*. New York, NY: Doubleday.

Vygotsky, L. S. (1978). *Mind in society: The development of higher psychological processes*. Cambridge, MA: Harvard University Press.

5

OBSERVING, PARTICIPATING, AND INVESTIGATING TEACHING PRACTICES

I want to understand the world from your point of view. I want to know what you know in the way you know it. I want to understand the meaning of your experience, to walk in your shoes, to feel things as you feel them, to explain things as you explain them. Will you become my teacher and help me understand?

(James P. Spradley)

We began this journey with relationship building. Your next moves into mentoring and coaching involve opening yourself up as a teacher and a learner. You will need to engage, reveal, and expose the pedagogical content knowledge (Shulman, 1986) that informs your teaching practices. The preservice teachers may begin on the periphery but they will become increasingly deeper and more involved over time. You will also need to be prepared to model the reflective practices that are essential to the CARE model. In the case of cooperating teachers and mentor teachers of beginning teachers, the expectations around representing and modeling your teaching will be fairly straightforward. In other coaching and mentoring situations, there may need to be some adjustments to the context you are working.

Analysis of Routines and Practices

Doing (modeling) and explicitly describing teaching practices are both forms of representing in the Grossman and McDonald (2008) version of supporting preservice teachers. As a mentor or coach you can certainly "do" your practices and have someone observe. You can describe your practices to someone in a form that might complement or enrich an observation. You can also go one step further by "deconstructing" these practices around the intentions and actions you take. We view the combination of these strategies as powerful in creating an entry space for the preservice teacher. You are not engaging the preservice teacher around a right or wrong way but rather around the way you have come to grow your practice. You will stress throughout that these practices are always under development.

Activity Configurations

We are going to suggest a plan for describing and deconstructing classroom teaching practices that has been useful in our work. Our plan is based on the innovation configurations that came out of the Concerns Based Adoption Model for professional learning (Hall and Loucks, 1977) (see also Chapter 3). However, we use the term Activity Configurations to emphasize the socially situated and practice-based approach we take to thinking about practices in the classroom. Activity Configurations are ways of making explicit for others the crafting of an activity structure and the content knowledge that undergirds these practices. Activity Configurations are not meant to cast our practices in stone. Rather, they are ways of clarifying our activities so that we can help others see inside what we do.

Practices are conceptual, behavioral, and intentional. Practices are experienced by the students in your classroom in routines of work that are conducted often, but not always, around subject areas. A teacher describing her practices might, for example, begin by describing the daily schedule. "We begin each morning with a community circle where we.... We have a language arts block from 9:30 to 11:30. We do mathematics from 1:00–1:45. We alternate science and social studies every two weeks."

If we pushed for a closer description we might see language arts time broken down into a reading/writing workshop, a daily read-aloud, and some guided reading. If we pushed further we might get some details on the parts in structures that move (e.g., in read-alouds, the books we choose for read-alouds or the comprehension strategies we focus on) and the parts that stay the same (the routines and participation structures for discussion and response; the tools we have access to in our workshop). The closer we push toward this description and the more we insert why kinds of questions as part of the conversation, the closer we get to creating a shared understanding of practices.

As an exercise, we are going to ask that you think about something you teach in your day, analyze the practice, and represent this practice for someone else. If you are not currently teaching, reach back into your past teaching and identify some routine part of your day in teaching. The first part of an Activity Configuration is a definition of **products**—the work that is being produced: What is the purpose and goal of the activity? In some ways, this part of the exercise helps us to orient ourselves to the reasons for our work in the classroom and we can begin to think about who we are serving when we do this activity.

Next, think of this practice in terms of what is **critical**: What parts of this teaching involve something you (and your students) do each and every time you are working in this activity? You will have to write or describe what is important in your thinking around that practice. For example, careful book selection that is considerate of a number of factors is critical to a quality read-aloud experience. What else is critical (for you)? Should the books being read be organized into units of study? How about the expression in your reading? The discussion? The response? How about how often and how long the read-alouds are? And on and on. We call these critical features—essential elements that need to be there for you to consider this your desired practice.

Consider the example of a reader's workshop. Ask your colleagues and almost everyone will claim that it is a practice they enact in their classroom. But the label of "workshop" may not tell or reveal important differences. When is a workshop a workshop and when is it not? (for you … you don't need to judge others). Are students free to choose what they write about and in what form? Will you offer a mini-lesson at the start? Will you meet to debrief at the end? What are you doing between the start and the finish as a teacher? Only you in your practice can identify what is critical and for each of these features you have a reason and a purpose that is compelling for you.

Now, think about features of this practice that are **optional**: These are the elements you sometimes include. So, you might like to have some kind of inquiry come out of each read-aloud. You might like to bring in background on the author that you might want to share. You might have a focus comprehension strategy. You might have some vocabulary goals drawing from the text. You might want them to do some writing out of the read-aloud that connects to the author's craft.

Finally, there are **variations** within each of these components that might range from the optimal to variations that might not be acceptable. As an example, your practice in language arts teaching is to use read-alouds. How often counts? Daily might be optimal for 30 minutes minimum. How about three times a week? How about five minutes? At what point does the variability cross a point of not really part of practice? Think of the statement, "We do a writer's workshop in our classroom." You discover this means 30 minutes on Friday afternoons. Does this count as doing a writing workshop? In the end, it is for the teacher to describe their practices. We offer an elaborate example of a read-aloud Activity Configuration in Appendix A and an additional blank version in Appendix B. This is the start of a deconstruction of a practice that allows someone to see into a practice what is intended (and even why) that complements the observation from the outside looking in. These kinds of documents create spaces for conversations around your thinking and your planning. This is some of the hardest work that a mentor and a coach have to do in supporting a preservice teacher.

Some might look at this kind of detailed representation as the beginning of a script to follow and a sort of fidelity template for teaching practices. This is not the intention at all. This deconstruction has to come from each teacher as reflecting his or her thinking. Initially there will be a lot mirroring and mimicking on the part of the novice as they move into teaching. You will hear your own voice. You will see your own movements as your novice appropriates these practices.

From the start, they want to be the kind of teacher you are. Moving forward they will want to become their own teacher. It is a process and a transition that you cannot rush or hurry them through. They will have to make that journey. What is important in representing your teaching practices is that you model them as changing and growing and evolving. The description of your teaching practices as critical features and what those might look like will change. This is one of the most important lessons you will teach as a mentor.

Sometimes the preservice teacher sees practices from the outside looking in and it appears to be all flow. Only your description of the struggles and challenges in teaching reveal the real work a teacher is doing. The best coach is often the one who struggled the most to achieve what they have as a teacher. Those who have struggled not only have empathy, they have insight into how to make what looks impossible from the outside as totally doable.

Shadowing

There is this image most of us hold about observing in a classroom. We find a space in the back, outside of the action zone, and do our best to not be noticed. We write furiously as we watch trying to capture everything that is happening. We have even been in schools that have an observation room to use for such observations. You observe through a one-way glass mirror in a separate room and thus are even able to talk with colleagues while watching. What if we changed the rules for observing? What if we changed our perspective entirely?

A few years ago, we worked with a cooperating teacher who didn't get the message about observing from afar. From the start, she told her student teacher: "You're with me. I've put you a chair right next to mine. If I move around you go with me. Don't let yourself get more than three feet away from me or you might miss something." We noticed several things as we watched this unfold over time. First, the preservice teacher was seeing what the teacher was seeing. The student teacher could "read" the same expressions the teacher was reading—not the backs of heads. Second, the cooperating teacher would often make important side comments (almost whispers) to the preservice teacher on what and why she was engaging in the ways she was. Third, the preservice teacher was positioned (physically) in teacher space and began to take on this as part of their identity. Think back now to the notion of "legitimate peripheral participation" we introduced in Chapter 3. This move was part of bringing the novice into practice.

We have come to regard this "shadowing" as a strategy for participation. We have encouraged this practice from the start as an important and powerful move for coming into practice. Both mentors and novices have reported that there is clearly an awkward stage of having someone "in your space" with you and feeling a bit chained together. But in almost all cases, the uncomfortable gives way to the normal way of doing teaching and mentoring along the way. This kind of side-by-side experience should become the norm not the exception. If the

FIGURE 5.1   Preservice Teacher Shadowing Her Cooperating Teacher

preservice teacher is in the room they should be at your side. Figure 5.1 shows both cooperating teacher and preservice teacher at the front of the class, side-by-side, during a read-aloud.

Purposeful Observations

There should be a special set of observation experiences where you (the mentor) take the lead in modeling reflection in practice. This is not a staged modeling but a real model for what you do all the time in your teaching practice. While the steps will not be as detailed as the steps described in the coming chapter for your observations of your preservice teacher, there is the intention here that connections will help them moving forward.

Here, your Activity Configurations become relevant again. What are some of the areas that you are ready to think about in this detail? Those are likely the most key components of your practice and may guide you in terms of where to begin. Pick something to start with from your daily routine. It could be a read-aloud, a math lesson, or a mini-lesson around writing. It could be whole class or small group or even individual (e.g., conferencing with students around writing). You might even invite the preservice teacher to choose where they would like to begin. Engage in close shadowing around this practice for a few days. Take time to explain what you are doing as you are doing it—sharing your Activity Configuration and even making revisions along the way as you discover more about the practice. Engage in conversation around the thinking beneath the practice. This means you will need to prepare: "This is what and why I do what I do in this Activity Configuration." You explain what is critical (essential) and optional as well as what you are striving for. It is important that you present the structure as something you have developed and are continuing to explore and work on. ("I am working to get better at guiding the group discussions." "I am working to offer think aloud in ways that are better connected to the comprehension strategies we are working on.") You have to position yourself as a learner in your teaching. In Appendix C of this book, we have shared with you a Purposeful Observation guide that we use with our preservice teachers.

Building on this base, the Purposeful Observation begins with a short pre-conference (less than five minutes). The preservice teacher already has some insight into the activity structure based on shadowing and explanation. The pre-conference is specific to the upcoming Purposeful Observation. You offer the preservice teacher a quick sketch for how you envision the teaching will unfold. You talk briefly around the challenges you anticipate for the children. You mention anything that you are working on in particular. You invite the preservice teacher to focus their observation on the kids' responses to the teaching (e.g., note patterns; capture interactions; perhaps even interview students after the teaching around the experience). All in five minutes.

Next the preservice teacher observes the teaching. Again, this does not have to be removed and in the back of the room. The observation can very well take place in a shadowing mode. There is total permission for the preservice teacher to take notes as they are observing, or the writing might occur later as a written reflection the preservice teacher makes based on what he or she noticed. In addition, you might consider having the preservice teacher videotape you during Purposeful Observations, and model the ways you use that video to look closer into your teaching.

Schedule some time later in the day or even the next day to discuss the observation. You will be doing a lot of the talking during this conversation. You will, in essence, be debriefing yourself around the experience. Talk about what you have been thinking about since the teaching. Talk about changes you made during the teaching that you had not anticipated making. Talk about things you learned through the lesson and want to take forward. Be critical. "I don't think I challenged the students enough in this lesson." Invite the preservice teacher to share the data they gathered and interact around that data.

These Purposeful Observations can be repeated many times in anticipation of the preservice teacher taking a turn in this activity structure in a lead role. They need to see the variability with each teaching event. As time moves forward, you might expand the Purposeful Observations into other Activity Configurations—from reading to writing workshop, for example. Every step in the process of the Purposeful Observation is intended to (a) reflect what teachers are doing all the time inside of their heads as teachers; and (b) set up for a role reversal as the novice moves into a lead teaching role. You may feel, in these Purposeful Observations, that you are doing most of the talking. That is perfectly OK. The role reversal will happen later and you will become the active listener.

Co-teaching

Co-teaching is an idea that has long been an alternative to the individualistic notions of the sole teacher in the room. Friend and Cook (1996) are often cited in references to co-teaching, and they offer four models of interactions that teachers might take in the classroom together. Think about where the teachers are in the room. Sometimes the teachers are side-by-side, and the teaching is "together." Other times, teachers are doing things in parallel—there may be two groups of students and each teacher is working with one group in the classroom. Other times, one teacher is "lead" and the other is working in support. These are all models to try and explore in your co-teaching with your preservice teacher.

We have emphasized from the start that you need to create a sense of "we" as the teachers in this classroom. The preservice teacher is not waiting in the wings to try out. You are a team. Yes, you are the more experienced teacher, but you are both learning and you are both responsible. Examine your discourse patterns. "We," not "I." "Our," not "mine." One important place to do this is by expanding the preservice teacher's role in the shadowing of teaching. They are not the invisible shadow. Engage them. "Ms. Simmons, would you mind charting some of the ideas the students are offering?" "Ms. Simmons what do you think about Jose's comment on the story?" "Well that surely is a puzzle. Ms. Simmons can you help us think through this?"

These are the kinds of small moves that will make the perceived giant next step of "now you teach and I'll watch" much less of an enormous hurdle than a small step into the lead. Co-teaching can expand and expand. Offer roles and activities in your teaching that involve the preservice teacher. Plan together for these co-teaching moments. Make it clear that the preservice teacher can and should feel free to step in and contribute ideas. We are deconstructing here the idea that there is a real and a pretend teacher in the classroom. We are going to co-invest so strongly into co-teaching that the students will not even know how to respond to the question: Who is the real teacher in this classroom?

Getting Preservice Teachers Ready for CARE

One of the biggest struggles we faced in our early work with the CARE model was the resistance we perceived from the preservice teachers. They wanted feedback. They wanted an expert telling them what to do and how to do it and when they were doing it well. What we had perceived as resistance, however, was not that as much as it was confusion and uncertainty. We failed in our work of introducing the model to include the preservice teachers in our model. Once we engaged them with the model, and how it works and why we found partners in the process, that put the focus on the real learning.

Don't make a secret of how and why you are going to coach them. Be direct and explicit. Help each other in making the model work. It will take both of you on the same page to succeed. Help catch each other when you find yourself falling into the evaluative mode. Just as an example, in the Purposeful Observations you might have the preservice teacher in the post-conference say something along the lines of: "I really liked the way…." You can respectfully appreciate the comment but redirect to focus on what he or she noticed, in particular about the students and their work. "Praise" given and received is addictive and mostly not empowering. It takes a lot of practice to move away from the need to give and receive praise. Your encouragement and your feedback on your teaching must come through the students you teach.

A final note about "feedback" ends this chapter. We have to show preservice teachers that the most important feedback they can get is from the students they teach while they are teaching. One of the most important jobs we have in mentoring and coaching is to help them attend to and make sense of the feedback the students are providing all of the time. The novice asks for feedback in the sense of evaluation ("Tell me what you liked." "Tell me how to improve."). We resist the temptation to answer these kinds of questions and instead turn the attention back to those who are served. "What did the kids teach you today?" "How did you attend to what they were telling you?" "What tools did you use to notice how they were responding?" Experience is our teacher if we are willing to and know how to examine experiences carefully.

One of the biggest challenges you, and your preservice teacher, will face is to eliminate the evaluative from your discourse patterns. "I liked the way…" or "I think you should have…." These are the kinds of statements that put you, the teacher, as the authority figure to be considered. It's sometimes a matter of rephrasing: not just being more specific but rephrasing in the shift to focus on the students. "I noticed when you did … the kids responded by…." The affirmation comes in recognizing what a preservice teacher is doing and how it is powerful.

Two Cases: Shift from Evaluation to Reflection

As we mentioned previously, when preservice teachers were intentionally included in conversations about this model, they demonstrated an understanding of the purpose of reflection in their development. They were then able to draw on these understandings to engage in reflective talk and thinking to support their development as teachers. Through reflective conversations with cooperating teachers, they began to recognize how reflection could be used as a tool to analyze their teaching and make changes to their practice.

Bianca completed her final two semesters of student teaching in a first grade classroom. The cooperating teacher, Ashley, had previous experience with leading professional development and supporting new teachers on her campus; however, this was her first assignment as a cooperating teacher. Bianca described the qualities she wanted in a cooperating teacher at the start of the year for a quick write in her literacy methods course. She wrote,

> I need someone who will be there in those moments that I decide to try something for the first time or when I decide to take risks and will help to think about what I did that worked or what I could improve on ... I need someone who will be willing to learn with and alongside me, and I would like a mentor who considers me a valuable asset to their classroom as much as they are valuable to me in my learning.

In the first sentence, we can see that Bianca ultimately wanted to work with a teacher that would "help [me] to think" and "learn with and alongside me"; these ideas supported Bianca's desire to have the space to reflect rather than be told. However, we can also see that Bianca did want guidance on "what I did that worked or what I could improve on," which seemed to indicate that Bianca positioned the cooperating teacher as the expert who could guide her towards teaching in ways that "work," which is common for preservice teachers. But, we also noticed that there was an inherent tension for Bianca in her desire to want a mutual relationship based on learning and respect, while at the same time, there was a desire to have someone catch her (possibly) before she falls.

As the year progressed, Ashley and Bianca learned about coaching with CARE in their university classes and with each other. At the end of her student teaching semester, Bianca recalled that through dialogue and reflection, she was able to appreciate herself more as a teacher,

> It also really helped me, because I'm really hard on myself, so normally I'm just like, "That was terrible." It helped me find ways to find the successes in every day too, which I think you need that in your everyday, after a hard day. "This went really well, and I'm going to take this and use it tomorrow." So I think that's one way that I've definitely become a better teacher, too.

By learning to reflect in and on practice, Bianca positioned herself as the classroom teacher by broadening her vision from the success or failure of a single lesson to the breadth and depth required to teach day after day. Through reflection, Bianca was able to appreciate her own learning as a process, rather than a product required to meet a fulfillment for the university or for the certification exam.

Preservice teachers and cooperating teachers both recognized the ways reflection allowed preservice teachers to view their practice from a different perspective and to develop without receiving praise or criticism from their cooperating teacher. In the following case, we meet Sylvia, preservice teacher, and Kimberly, cooperating teacher. They worked together as fifth grade language arts teachers. Sylvia and Kimberly recognized that reflection allowed them the opportunity to unpack complex moments and interpret the events from multiple perspectives. Together, as they reflected on practice, they were able to shed new light on the events that had occurred and move forward in a manner that was responsive to both the students and the teachers. At the end of her student teaching semester, Sylvia expressed why she felt that act of reflection was helpful,

> I was able to question my teaching practice and have, you know, have talk and discussions about this stuff. Maybe think about things I wouldn't have thought about before. Thinking, trying to make my lessons more student-centered, and how that affected my students, rather than just getting my point across, was really helpful. [Final interview, 2014]

Through reflection, Sylvia was able to take her mind off of her own requirements as a preservice teacher, and redirect her focus on the students. From the very beginning of CARE, we have done our best to keep the students at the heart of our work because then and only then can teachers begin to realize the impact they have each day. It was necessary for Kimberly that Sylvia learned to appreciate her efforts as the classroom teacher, as she appreciated the efforts of her students. Kimberly shared with us,

> She [Sylvia] also was very critical of herself and her practice. Very critical. When she saw me position it in a different way from what she was viewing it as, her eyes got big. She was just like, "Oh! I never thought of it that way!" And so she started to do some of that same regrouping that I did. Like, "Okay. Take a step back. Stop being so hard on the moment. What is working right here?" It's like flipping the coin. She started looking at it differently as well and I think it gave her a boost of confidence actually. She started to think about things very differently after those moments.

Kimberly approached her coaching and mentoring of Sylvia with the same purposefulness she approached teaching her fifth graders. Kimberly knew that often we are our own worst critics, and when we can recognize our own potential and strengths, then we are on the road to independence. Kimberly aimed to guide Sylvia to her own understandings.

Some Thinking and Talking To Do

- What are the areas you can see yourself working in first in terms of articulating an Activity Configuration? Second? What might come later in your work with your preservice teacher? Why do you think you have ordered your work this way?

- Shadowing might feel very awkward at first—teaching is usually very solitary work. How does it feel to teach with a partner?
- What is different about shadowing than "normal" observing? How is it more powerful? What is lost? Talk with your preservice teacher about his or her experience.
- What other steps can you take to build the practice of thinking of the classroom as "our" classroom, and "we" are the teachers?

References

Friend, M. and Cook, L. (1996). *Interactions: Collaboration skills for school professionals.* White Plains, NY: Longman.

Grossman, P. and McDonald, M. (2008). Back to the future: Directions for research in teaching and teacher education. *American Educational Research Journal,* 45(1), 184–205.

Hall, G. E. and Loucks, S. F. (1977). A developmental model for determining whether the treatment is actually implemented. *American Educational Research Journal,* 14(3), 263–276.

Shulman, L. S. (1986). Those who understand: Knowledge growth in teaching. *Educational Researcher,* 15, 4–14.

6

THE COACHING WITH CARE CYCLE

The Pre-conference and Observation

The interesting thing about coaching is that you have to trouble the comfortable, and comfort the troubled.

(Ric Charlesworth, hockey coach)

We have introduced the CARE model in terms of some theoretical and conceptual underpinnings. These earlier chapters are foundational for us in that they inform the "why" of our work. In the next several chapters we will describe the "how" of our work with preservice teachers using the CARE model in practice. Our fundamental belief is that preparing teachers to learn through practice is something that will serve them throughout their professional lives. As we grow professionally our "how" informs our "why" as we grow in our understanding of practice. As with all good theory, there is nothing linear or causal, only interactive and connected.

The assumption we make moving forward is that all the groundwork for mentoring and coaching discussed in the earlier chapters is established and will continue to be nourished with your preservice teacher. Relationships must be sustained. A relationship that is not growing is ending. Just as you are working on your relationship, you must also attend to the relationship the preservice teacher is building with the students in the class. Relationship building is one of the many places where the work we do as a mentor and coach with our preservice teachers parallels the kind of work that teachers do with students in the classroom all of time.

We also assume that at least a few of the Purposeful Observation routines described in the previous chapter have been completed. Keep in mind that these Purposeful Observations routines will continue as the preservice teacher moves into new content and new routines. In other words, you should plan for simultaneous practice work. The preservice teacher may be moving into independence in teaching in one area of the curriculum while she is just moving into a new curriculum area or Activity Configuration with co-teaching and Purposeful Observations.

In terms of planning ahead, it may be helpful for you to map out the plans for involvement for the month ahead or even for the entire semester. We have seen pacing guides constructed in this manner as very helpful and anxiety reducing. Example pacing guides are located in Appendix D. We encourage you to think of these pacing guides as flexible. Adjustments will likely be needed as momentum builds and challenges are faced. We also see these kinds of pacing guides as highly particular to a classroom setting. The Activity Configurations are unique to classrooms and teachers. There is no way to plan for such a guide that is appropriate across all classrooms.

The goal is to get the preservice teacher in a place where his or her feet are firmly on the ground in the classroom and well inside the mentor's head drawing on Purposeful Observations, shadowing and co-teaching experiences. We work toward saturation of experience to build confidence, and we rely on the preservice teacher to be involved in the decisions around doing more Purposeful Observations or taking the next step into practice. The CARE cycle of coaching is designed to support these next steps into teaching.

The CARE Coaching Cycle

The coaching cycle has these components, as pictured in Figure 6.1:

Reflecting into Practice (pre-conference)
Reflecting in Practice (observation/teaching practice)
Reflecting on Practice (post-conference)
Reflecting for Practice (post-conference and planning conference)

Not pictured in our model is the reflection that occurs outside the four contexts—what we might think of as reflecting around practice. We fully realize that teachers within the CARE model are constantly reflecting, and reflections outside of these components are part of thoughtfully adaptive teaching (Fairbanks et al., 2009).

This chapter will focus on the first two components in the cycle, the pre-conference and observation. Chapter 7 will address the post-conference and planning.

We will offer some guidance and suggestions for supporting your preservice teacher and even some language to explore in working with them. We stress, however, that all of these suggestions are offered as jumping-off points for you to explore in constructing your own coaching practices. It is only through the experience of doing and reflecting with your colleagues that this model will grow into a practice. The series of conferences that are part of the cycle are designed to tap into the thinking (cognitive) and feeling (emotional) dimensions of teaching practices. For the moment, we are going to think of these as conversations between you and the preservice teacher you are working with—although we will come back later to disrupt this assumption and consider some alternatives.

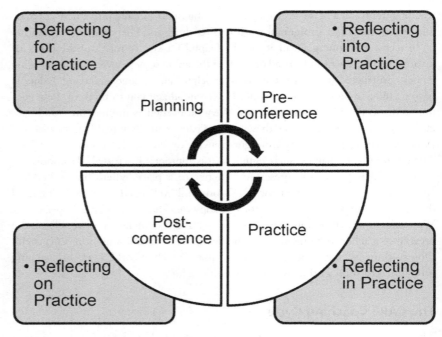

FIGURE 6.1 CARE Coaching Cycle

We have some general suggestions for all the conferences and we will become more specific as we move into each of the different conferences.

Space

We recommend conferring in a place that is free from distraction and noise. (We understand that this can be very difficult in elementary schools.) Try to schedule meetings that allow you to spend as much time as needed with room for flexibility. Body language, non-verbal clues, space, and physical activity are critical in enacting successful coaching practices. It can be difficult in a school, but try to find a space for your conferences where there is privacy and minimal outside disruptions—we have seen this happen in classrooms, in small nooks throughout the building, libraries, or even a borrowed specialist's office (see Figure 6.2).

For the conference try to take a position face-to-face, with shoulders square to each other. Anything physical between you (e.g., a desk, a notebook, a computer) tends to get in the way of connected physical space. Work to maintain eye-to-eye contact throughout the conferences. Leaning in is important. Open body language is important (no crossed arms or legs). It's often hard to find a time when you're not eating, because teachers' breaks are often at mealtime, but it is best if the primary focus is on the talk. In general, we discourage note taking—or if there is note taking it is for very specific purposes. The only papers on the table should

FIGURE 6.2   Preservice Teacher and Cooperating Teacher during a CARE Coaching Cycle Conference

be observational notes (data) that the coach has planned to reference during the conference.

Talk

The patterns of talk (e.g., participation, word choice, positions taken) in reflective conferences are crucial to examine. Every question you ask, every invitation you make to share something should be directly related to the kinds of questions and meta-talk that teachers do on their own as they reflect on teaching practices. The preservice teacher will be doing most of the talking in all of the conferences—a very rough guide for you in terms of the success of the conference. More success means less talking from the coach. You need to use active listening strategies and plenty of wait time. Slowing down creates more space for thinking.

You will see that we build repetition in the kinds of talk we suggest. This repetition is purposeful. We want the preservice teacher to come into the conference anticipating what will be asked. They will, after repeated engagements, begin to ask these questions of themselves and gain independence in their thinking. You will come to discover that, over time, you will not have to ask any of the questions posed here. The preservice teachers will incorporate these and anticipate these in their reflection processes.

Data

Almost everything that occurs around the CARE cycle can be viewed as data (e.g., notes, student work, video recordings, etc.). Examining these data can be extremely important in shaping the reflective processes. Most of what happens in the conferences and teaching is moving by very quickly. We need a means to capture data for review purposes. We are enthusiastic about the potential for video recordings as a tool for learning in reflective practice. In Chapter 10, we expand on some ways to actively use videos as part of the conferencing with preservice teachers. For now, we want to focus on video recording as a tool for you to use in your own professional development work in coaching. The video recordings of conferences create a space for you to inspect and reflect on your own coaching practices. The technology has become so accessible and flexible this kind of recording is much less of a challenge than in the past.

We have created a small guide to covering the technical side of video recording that appears in Appendix E of this book. We are not advocating for the production of some award winning movie, but rather a recording that is easy to store, easy to access, and easy to search. You can use your phone, a tablet, your computer, or a full camera set-up. As we guide you through the various conference types, we will suggest some specific video strategies.

The preservice teacher may be a bit nervous about the video recording at first. There are some specific things that you can do to minimize any apprehensions he or she may have. First, be clear on the purpose and that is for you to use in reflecting and growing your own coaching practices. In addition, you might consider having the preservice teacher videotape you during Purposeful Observations, and model the ways you think about your practice through video. Second, explain to the preservice teacher who will see this video—perhaps just you as the coach or perhaps a small group of teachers who are working together to study coaching. Be clear that no one else will have access to these videos and they will be destroyed at the end of your time working together. You may also offer copies of the videos to the preservice teacher if they are building a professional portfolio.

The students in your classroom may also find the video recording distracting. The more discrete you can be about the recording, the better. The more often you have the recorder turned on, the more the students will become accustomed to it. Finally, you will need to consider the ethics and permission processes around any of the students in your class who may appear in these videos. Most school districts have very specific requirements and procedures in place. As long as the videos are used for promoting growth in teaching and are not shared outside of the immediate context in which you are working, this is not a difficult process. In Appendix F, we offer a draft version of a "letter to parents" that has been used in some school districts. Again, you should be sure to check with your district regarding policies in place.

Of course, data can take other forms that are just as useful as video. There are the notes you take as part of your observation. There are the student work artifacts associated with the teaching. There are the planning documents and the resources used in the teaching. There are reflective notes or journal entries that may have been created after a lesson. We will think of the potential for all these data to inform our reflective processes.

Taking on the Lead Teaching Role

The CARE coaching cycle is applied in the context of the preservice teacher taking on a leading role in a teaching practice. This move is a step beyond the general observing, Purposeful Observations, and initial co-teaching that has been going on up to this point in time. As the cooperating teacher, you may be involved in this teaching. We don't want to create the image of the cooperating teacher leaving the room or hiding in the corner taking notes while the preservice teacher steps up.

For example, in Figure 6.3, the cooperating teacher and the preservice teacher are each working with a small group of students. During the planning conference or pre-conference, the preservice teacher may request, "When we break into group work, I would like for you to work with this group doing ... while I am working with other students." These kinds of arrangements reflect what the preservice has been doing with you through the start of your work together. The roles may be shifting but you are still, and will be, two teachers in the classroom supporting the students.

FIGURE 6.3   Preservice Teacher and Cooperating Teacher Co-teaching

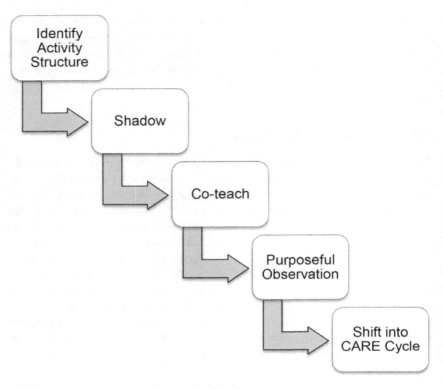

FIGURE 6.4 Entry into CARE Coaching Cycle

Our entry point into the CARE model, for the purposes of this book, is from the Activity Configuration experience into the point of the pre-conference as seen in Figure 6.4. Together with your preservice teacher, you will have identified an area of teaching that you might focus on initially. This will be an activity structure that you may have shared via an Activity Configuration, and the preservice teacher will have shadowed, co-taught and done Purposeful Observations around this activity structure.

It is now their turn to take the lead. Of course, planning is a precursor to the pre-conference; however, we want to emphasize that planning comes out of a post-conference and the action plan the cycle generates, thus we address it in the next chapter.

The Pre-conference: Reflecting into Practice

The pre-conference serves many functions. First, the pre-conference draws on the literature on teaching that suggests teachers operate from a mental image of a teaching experience that they are moving into. Think of yourself in your teaching life. There is that moment of entering the room or coming out of a transition where you are "ready." You take that deep breath and carry on. This teaching image is what is used to form expectations for flow of student and teacher work. The teaching almost never unfolds along the expected lines.

There are almost always surprises and challenges to respond to. The teaching image is helpful for the teacher in being responsive to these moments. We want to encourage the creation of these images that are as much about how things will look and sound as they are about content. This image is filled with plans for flow and activity in the teaching. The pre-conference is an opportunity to tap into that image and examine its qualities. The pre-conference is short and it happens as close to the actual teaching as possible in order to tap into the teaching image and not the planning processes; ten minutes or so before teaching is perfect. In most cases, you will already have a sense of what the teaching is going to be like. You are looking for just a quick image check on the teaching.

Some Suggested Invitations to Talk in the Pre-conference

You might begin with something as simple as, "Tell me about the work you will be doing with our students. Talk me through (very briefly) from start to finish." You will note that the focus is not on what you are going to see the preservice teacher doing but what they are going to be doing with the students. This is part of the effort to build the attention on the students and the work they will be doing. We do not focus here on the "objective" for the teaching (that is part of the work of planning) nor do we use the term "lesson" because this term suggests a certain form of teaching. We need the language to be open to possibilities. One of the follow-up questions to this starting place may be with respect to describing movement or shifts in the participation structure during the teaching. So, a teaching event might move from whole class to independent work and then back to the whole group. These transition points might be good to identify in preparation for your observation.

A second conversation space should be around the challenge that the preservice teacher expects the students to have inside of the teaching. This notion of challenge and struggle are essential to teaching and learning. The preservice teacher tends to want to reduce struggle as a means of securing high levels of participation and success. Deep engagement and learning come with struggle so we expect the answer from the preservice teacher to articulate the important points of struggle. This will be an important space for you to use in focusing during the observation and in the post-conference.

One of the cautions to consider is that the pre-conference should not turn into a planning conference. So if the conversation moves in the direction of, "I'm not too sure about this part of the teaching. Do you think I should do X or Y?" This is a move into planning and you don't want to engage with planning in the pre-conference. If you feel the uncertainty around the plan is too high, then you might want to suggest a move to co-teaching or that the teaching be postponed in order to develop a plan that is ready to go.

Toward the closing of the pre-conference, there are two important focus points you will want to ask the preservice teacher. First, "What or who do you want me to focus on while I am observing the teaching?" and "What data would you like for me to collect?" This is essentially the work you are being assigned to do. Preservice teachers will grow to anticipate these two questions and will be ready. At the start, they may need for you to suggest a few possibilities. "I could focus on some particular students and their work." "I could focus on the use of manipulatives in the activity." "I could focus on these students' participation in discussion." This will become easier to see when we describe the action plans the teacher is developing inside of the later points in the cycle. The essential point here is that your observation focus is on the students not on the preservice teacher's behavior. The feedback is coming from the students to the teacher and your observation will help them see student responses as cues for their responsive teaching and learning.

Secondly, especially because your focus may have been on co-teaching, is the question, "What would you like my role to be in the classroom?" (e.g., observe a particular group; scribe while students are talking, etc.) You may be asked to be working with students in some way (even shadowing your preservice teacher!). Stay open to these possibilities.

The final part of the pre-conference is to settle on a signal between you in terms of you stepping in to assist in the teaching. You may have already established a process for doing this in the planning stage but a reminder here is a good idea to place moving into teaching. It's not really helpful to think of these moves into teaching as "sink or swim" or "I'll only step in if there is danger of someone getting injured or the teaching is just a total disaster." It's far better to assure the preservice teacher that you are there and ready to move into co-teaching if that is what she feels is needed in the moment. The signal can range from a special look to a spoken invitation. "Ms. Jones would you like to come up here with me and we can explain the work ahead together." This is not a matter of failure but of a scaffold to success.

Four or five invitations to talk in the pre-conference and just a few minutes. That is all that is needed.

The Observation: Reflecting in Practice

Think of your work in the observation as a data gatherer. You will bring data to the discussion after the teaching. Figure 6.5 suggests possibilities for data collection. First, there is a general rule here that the data is drawing on the students' work, not on the teacher's behavior. This may seem a bit odd as a guide but consider what you are trying to accomplish. Our goal is to prepare the preservice teacher in learning through practice. They really can't observe themselves but they can be observant of their students and learn through them.

Second, you want to keep the appreciative frame in mind as you are gathering data. The most important data is data that reveals success for the students. Focus on the powerful moments of teaching. You will find the conversations that grow out of this data much more useful than data that focuses on shortcomings.

Some observers like to use a T-chart, as was suggested for the Purposeful Observation in the previous chapter. The T-chart creates space for description on the left side (low-inference data) and for interpretation on the right side (questions, noticings of patterns). If you are videotaping, do not walk around with your video-recording device. Just put it in one place that can capture most of what is going on. This will be sufficient for now.

There is likely the need for some response—a smile, even a thumbs-up or a quick hug. However, refrain from anything that approaches evaluation. "I am really looking forward to thinking about your teaching and talking through this experience with you."

Possible Data Collection Points:	Create a map that logs the times and significant transition points within the teaching. This data may be useful as you consider issues around lesson flow and time management.
	Script exchanges between students and students or the teachers and students. Don't judge, just transcribe.
	Note moments of surprise or changes from what you thought was planned for the teaching.
	Note body language and body movement. Focus on changes of expression in the teacher or the students that suggest some kind of mental activity.
	If students are working independently or in small groups, move around and talk to the students about what they are doing and why.
	Watch for moments of challenge and struggle for the students. Focus, in particular, on those moments that were resolved to the student's satisfaction. Focus on just a few students not all of them.
	Gather artifacts from the teaching that represent the work of the students. If possible you can keep a copy or take a photo of student work to share with the preservice teacher.
	Interview a few students after the teaching. "What was your work about today?" "How did you do?" "What was helpful?" "What was a challenge?"

FIGURE 6.5   Points of Observation

Transitioning to the Post-conference

We will go into detail around the post-conference in the next chapter. For the purposes of closure in this chapter, we just want to suggest that the post-conference be delayed. Teaching for the novice can be very anxiety provoking or draining emotionally or even creating a highly positive response state. There is important processing time needed for the preservice teacher to make sense of the experience. How long? One hour is likely not enough. One day is good. Two or three days of delay from the observation may be getting too far removed from the experience for rich discussion. There is no absolute and contexts will vary. However, it is clear from our work that delay really helps the quality of the conversation in the post-conference.

A Case: A Pre-conference Using the CARE Cycle

Here we introduce Helen, cooperating teacher, and Renee, preservice teacher, to take us through the CARE cycle in this chapter and the following chapter. Helen and Renee worked together as first grade ESL teachers for an entire school year, and they engaged in nine formal coaching with CARE cycles across the academic year. We will share a CARE cycle from the fall semester, in which Renee taught a mini-lesson on poetry and word work and supported students as they read independently during reading workshop. The following transcript is of the pre-conference Helen and Renee had before Renee taught her lesson. It has been edited, but provides a look at how a pre-conference might unfold in real-time. It was a total of six minutes in length. We have emboldened phrases that Helen used that reflect the coaching moves we might expect to see in a pre-conference.

> **Helen: Tell me a little bit about what we are going to see.**
>
> **Renee:** We are doing the poetry lesson. We will see the kids read the poem aloud with me, following along with their finger or pencil as they read. And then the students will also read independently.
>
> **Helen: Do you want to share step-by-step?**
>
> **Renee:** I am going to call the kids to the carpet. The kids will bring their poetry notebooks and a pencils. I am going to read the poem aloud, and I will ask them to point out the rhyming words in the poem. As part of our word work, we will also talk about different words in the poems and different sounds and parts of words (e.g., long /i/, there is = there's, definition of "slobbered"). After that, we will read the poem together in slow motion, and then I'll have them come up with two different voices to read it in. Then they will choose a voice to read in independently. While they are reading independently in their own voice and at their own pace, I will walk around and listen in to get an idea of what they are doing with the poem.

Helen: During that part, will you confer with the kids? When you are working with the whole group, **what do you want me to look for?** What are some of the actions that I can look for to know that the students understand?

Renee: I am looking to see that they are following along with their pencil or their finger. I am going have them box the rhyming words—we'll see if they are actually boxing and marking things that I mark up on the overhead as we talk about them.

Helen: So, you are planning to check if they are actively engaged in what you are doing in whole group as well. What about when they are reading independently? You will be conferring with them, **but what would you like my role to be?** I can also confer with them, if you like.

Renee: Yeah, that would be great.

Helen: OK, **what do you want me to look for** when I am conferring with the kids?

Renee: I want to know if they are actually reading the words, or are they following along with someone next to them. I want to understand *how* independently they are reading.

Helen: How do you feel about them reading with a partner? Or would you prefer for them to be reading independently?

Renee: I think it is fine if they are reading with a partner. I don't know if I want to start with partner reading.

Helen: If I notice them reading with a partner on their own, then it is OK?

Renee: Yeah. I don't want to discourage it because it is probably a support they are using.

Helen: Exactly.

Renee: If there are kids that want to read independently and feel confident reading independently, or if they are reading with a partner, they are both fine with me.

Helen: That is really good clarification. **Where do you think the students might struggle in this activity?**

Renee: I think possibly with the words themselves. The word "slobber" is going to probably be kind of a challenging idea. And I want to make sure that everyone understands it. The long /i/ sound and the bossy "e" that tells the "o" to say its name may feel confusing for some of them.

Helen: How can we support them if they are struggling?

Renee: Just going over and conferring with the student one-to-one in order to get a better idea of what s/he is understanding, and maybe partner the student up at that point with someone whose understanding is more and have the peer explain the idea.

Helen: Definitely. I can try that out when I am conferring with them too. **Are there any students in particular that you want me to focus on?**

Renee: I would like to focus on Evan and Katie.

Helen: Also, **is there anything you want me to look for in the data you want me to collect?**

Renee: Student engagement. I want to make sure that they are engaged in the ways I kind of expect.

Helen: Engagement is the primary focus, as well as focusing on Evan and Kate. I feel like we have a pretty good understanding of what I am going to be doing as I confer with them. And I understand the step-by-step of our lesson. **I am excited to see how it is going to turn out.**

Renee: OK! Me too.

This transcript provides a very clear map of the architecture of the pre-conference. Helen began with, "Tell me a little bit about what we are going to see," and followed with a request for a "step-by-step." You might also use the phrase, "Walk me through it." Twice in the pre-conference, Helen uses the phrases, "What do you want my role to be?" prompting Renee to think about the co-teaching roles in the classroom. She prompts Renee to think about what data she would like Helen to collect, using several phrases. The first two are general—asking what she should watch for in her conferring and in general, in the data. She also asks about specific students. Finally, she ends the pre-conference with a positive, forward-looking statement. What is amazing, and significant, is the amount of reflecting into practice that Renee is doing in this conference. Even though the planning had been done beforehand, we imagine that the design of the work was much clearer and Renee felt ready to teach after this short conversation.

Some Thinking and Talking To Do

- What is the status of the preservice teacher's relationship with the students in the class? Preservice teachers often struggle with finding a relationship that is personal, trusting, and caring but still professional.
- What conversations or actions can you initiate that ensure a positive working relationship in the classroom? One important place to start is in the preservice teachers' participation and leadership in daily class meetings.
- How do you decide when the preservice teacher is ready to take the lead in a teaching routine that they have been observing and co-teaching? To what degree should they make that decision?
- The use of data to inform decision-making has become a major focus in professional development work. Too often, data is limited to a consideration of test scores. Through the use of video and the study of work artifacts we are hoping to expand the notion of data to be broader and more inclusive.

In what ways do you use data in your own classroom to support your personal reflection processes? Do you have any favorite tools or processes?

- How do you plan? What records for planning do you create? How is this process helpful to you in your teaching? How has your planning changed as you have become more experienced in your teaching? You might explore your responses to these questions with your preservice teacher.
- With the pre-conference, we are introducing some very specific probes. How do you engage with these probes without sounding scripted? How do you make these words and phrases part of a conversation and not an interrogation? In part the answer rests in a deep understanding of why these invitations are being asked. In part the answer rests in helping the preservice teachers see the spaces tapped into by these questions as fundamental to learning through teaching.

Reference

Fairbanks, C. M., Duffy, G. G., Faircloth, B. S., He, Y., Levin, B, Rohr, J. et al. (2009). Beyond knowledge: Exploring why some teachers are more thoughtfully adaptive than others. *Journal of Teacher Education, 61*(1–2), 161–171.

7

THE COACHING WITH CARE CYCLE

The Post and the Planning Conferences

Listening is such a simple act. It requires us to be present, and that takes practice, but we don't have to do anything else. We don't have to advise, or coach, or sound wise. We just have to be willing to sit there and listen.

(Margaret J. Wheatley)

On some days, we want to say that the post-conference is the most important phase in the CARE coaching cycle. But we generally want to say the same thing when we are talking about any of the other phases. For now, we will just put the post-conference at the crucial middle space between what happened (or what we think happened) and what we will plan for moving forward. What is clear is that there is a lot of work for the preservice teacher and the cooperating teacher to do in preparation for the post-conference. This is one of the many reasons why the delay between the teaching and the post-conference is so important. The time is necessary for the preservice teacher to process the experience and for the mentor teacher to plan for the post-conference.

Preparing for the Post-conference

Some of our cooperating teachers have taken to sharing the notes they took during the observation with the preservice teacher in advance of the post-conference. These are non-evaluative notes that represent the data collected by the cooperating teacher. While we respect this strategy, we are cautious in recommending the sharing of observation notes for fear that these notes might shape the preservice teacher's processing of the experience. The preservice teacher may be in the mode of trying to read into the notes what the cooperating teacher thinks is important. What we want to learn through the post-conference is what information and what parts of the experience were high in the consciousness of the preservice teacher and why.

Costa and Garmston (1994) write about the need for a coach to have a road map for a post-conference something along the lines of a game plan that a coach might have anticipating a difficult opponent. We view this game planning as essential to a good post-conference. A game plan is constructed around main points (or "big ideas") to be addressed and some plans for contingencies. The main points that are targeted should come from an appreciative stance (i.e., these are things to notice and build on and make more powerful in your teaching) and not from a deficit view (i.e., these are the most important things to fix). This shift from deficit to appreciative can be challenging as we have all been shaped over the years to prioritize fixing things that are broken. In the application of the CARE model we are working to disrupt and replace this deficit view and substitute a more powerful plan.

The road map needs to be constructed around data gathered from your observation of students, or from the dialogue between the teacher and the students, or from interviews you conducted with students, or from a close examination of the work artifacts produced during the teaching. In addition to the main focus points the road map must also include provisions for contingencies. "If the preservice teacher says ... then I will.... If the preservice teacher doesn't raise ... then I will approach the topic by...." Your work is to first create space for the preservice teacher to reflect. You want to know their thinking and where it is taking them. If you just jump in with your main points, then you will have missed the opportunity to understand how they are thinking and processing.

There is no single format that the road map should take. It is often a good idea to have sketched out the main points you want to address and then have some plan for introducing these points through the data you have collected. The most important thing is that there is a thread tying the post-conference together, and the road map helps you to keep the main idea in focus. You might think about where you envision the conference ending—with a clear action—and working backwards. We offer an example of a cooperating teacher's road map in Figure 7.1 including an open invitation, sharing of student data, a discussion of choices made through reflection in action, puzzling together through a moment, and providing space to include other concerns of the preservice teacher. Note the appreciative focus related to the main points, the connection with the data gathered, and the plan for introduction.

In a perfect world, the novice will talk reflectively during the post-conference through the experience looking back and looking forward on the points of real significance in teaching with almost no need for direction from you. In a perfect world, you may never even use one of the prompts you have identified in your road map. Now that's success. In the real world, you need to be ready when this doesn't happen or goes in a direction you didn't anticipate. That's when and why a road map is so valuable.

It is important that the preservice teacher understand their work in preparing for the post-conference as well. The main work is in identifying the things

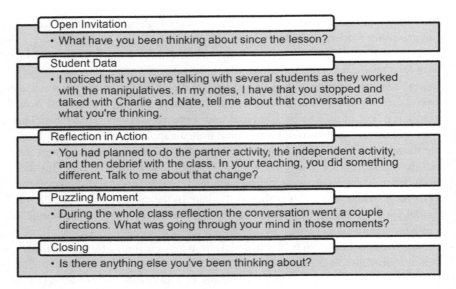

Open Invitation
• What have you been thinking about since the lesson?

Student Data
• I noticed that you were talking with several students as they worked with the manipulatives. In my notes, I have that you stopped and talked with Charlie and Nate, tell me about that conversation and what you're thinking.

Reflection in Action
• You had planned to do the partner activity, the independent activity, and then debrief with the class. In your teaching, you did something different. Talk to me about that change?

Puzzling Moment
• During the whole class reflection the conversation went a couple directions. What was going through your mind in those moments?

Closing
• Is there anything else you've been thinking about?

FIGURE 7.1 Example of a Cooperating Teacher's Road Map

that they want to talk about with you—things that happened and things that didn't happen that they might not have anticipated. Here again, preservice teachers are like anyone else in their wanting to talk about what didn't go well and how to fix it. We need to remind them that our focus is appreciative. "Come ready to talk about things you have been thinking through since your teaching. Be sure to focus on things we can we build on moving forward." They may want to take notes. That's fine. Here again, suggest that they focus their thinking on the data that they processed during the teaching. "What was said?" "What was done?" Focus on the details and the moments not on global impressions or generalizations.

The Post-conference: Reflecting on Practice

Recall our recommendations of space when you are beginning the post-conference—this is the time when it matters most that you're face to face. You may want to video record this post-conference so you can bring it back to a community of coaches you're working with. If so, set the laptop so that it captures you and the preservice teacher—not just one person. It will be important to see body language and use of materials in the video.

We generally suggest that the cooperating teacher start with a very open-ended invitation to share. "I know you have been thinking a lot about the teaching experience yesterday. Tell me what you have been thinking about, or what's been on your mind." Alternatively, even if it's for the sake of variety, you might want to begin by exploring their emotional and affective state. "How are you feeling about the experience?" We try to stay away from questions like,

"How did it go?" as this puts the student in an evaluative (albeit self-evaluative) position. We want to minimize the evaluative and maximize the reflection through the experience. Use invitations like, "Let's talk more about that." Or, "Can you elaborate a little on that moment?" Wait time is always important. You can lead topic changes using simple statements. "What else have you been thinking about?"

If the opportunity presents itself, and it will, then bring in the data you gathered that relates to a point that the preservice teacher has made. A comment from the preservice teacher about a particular student's response to a story, for example, might elicit from you a quote you have in your notes. Here is a case where bringing your notes into the conversation is totally appropriate. You may have transcribed a part of a dialogue. Share that as something to think and talk about. You may very well find that most of the points you had planned in your road map come up very naturally in the conversation.

There are two key coaching moves that we have learned from the cooperating teachers with whom we have worked. The first is the phrase, "Let's slow down that moment." We will return to this phrase in Chapter 11, focused on using video in the post-conference. But you don't need video to re-enter a teaching event and think about who was there, what was happening, and how the event unfolded in order to reflect.

The second move we learned began with the preservice teacher lamenting a choice she made in her teaching. The coach made the move to say, "When you did … that was a choice. What other choices were possible?" This move functioned to help the preservice teacher see that we are always considering new possibilities in our teaching—it is part of being thoughtfully adaptive. Also asking, "What happened?" "What adjustments did you make? How did these work for you?" can help to encourage this kind of reflection.

At times, you might refer back to what he or she said in the pre-conference as a way to open conversations about adaptive teaching. You might point back to something that was explicit in the plan but did not find its way into the teaching. Try not to make this a gotcha moment but rather recognition that we are always adapting our teaching. Don't limit the thinking around these moments as negative—they can create a wonderful path into appreciative reflection and learning.

You are entering a territory in this conversation that may be difficult. You might come up against: "What could I or should I have done at that point?" or, it's corollary, "What would you have done?" You don't want to engage with either of these questions. You really don't know what you would have done because you were not in the situation leading into that moment. It may be really hard for you to not just go ahead and tell them what you think, but that doesn't enhance their decision-making. One shift you can make is to focus not on the "should have" but on the "could have." You can shift this kind of probe into a more positive direction by thinking about (even brainstorming) what options were available to you at that moment and what might the consequences have been. This path reflects what we do in teaching all the time. We consider possibilities and we make the best choices we can and move on.

Once you have explored these adaptations, you will want to explore some other data from the pre-conference such as the challenge point for the students. We want to encourage preservice teachers to understand that challenge is essential to learning. If the students were not challenged in the lesson, then the learning opportunities were pretty small. Use the post-conference to celebrate challenges that were present, to notice that there may have been management issues but these can be resolved in ways that don't involve removing challenge. Inside these conversations around changes you made, again, should bring in any data that might support positive reflection.

Another important strategy that is part of your coaching repertoire is the attention you give to the noticing, naming, and the extending of strategies. This is particularly important as you enact your appreciative focus. "I noticed that you ... and the student(s) responded with..." (invite the preservice teacher to comment). You might name that strategy (e.g., scaffolding) and then extend the strategy in some ways (e.g., these are temporary supports that we must plan to remove as the student becomes more independent). These noticing, naming, and extending actions bring the preservice teacher deeper into the professional knowledge base of teaching and provide connections that can lead to even deeper thinking. "You were picking up on Jonas's questions in the discussion. I have a nice article I will share with you that talks about children's questioning and building an inquiry curriculum. I'd love to talk with you about it in thinking about our classroom."

If a topic has not been brought up that clearly should have been in your mind, then you can begin to use your data selectively. Try to stay focused on the appreciative:

> I noticed when you ... Jason did this....
> When I spoke to a couple of the students after the teaching this is what they said. What do you think?
> Let's look at some of the work artifacts from the students and try to make some sense of what was going on and their learning.

Try to engage the student more around problem-posing than problem-solving. Problem-solving often leads us to focus on fixing things. Problem-posing leads us to questions and dialogue that really empower teaching.

You have made it this far into the post-conference without using judgment or praise. That's progress. You need to take those urges toward praising and liking and turn them into appreciation statements. This is valuing of the work the preservice teacher has done that is the most important feedback they can use.

Toward the end of the post-conference you will want to have a conversation around growth. "How did your students grow? How did you grow?" We have found that growth tends to get a broader and richer range of responses than asking about "learning." Start with the students. Relate the comments made around growth to what was expressed in the pre-conference. Sometimes we are surprised by growth in areas we may not have identified going into the teaching. It can be the same conversation around the preservice teacher's growth. We expect learning through every teaching experience. Even small things count and accumulate into big things.

Finally, you will want to bring the conference to a close with a conversation around an action plan. The preservice teacher might have already articulated something that he or she wants to take forward into teaching, or maybe not. The action plan has two parts. In the first part, we are making decisions about next steps. Perhaps the preservice teacher wants to continue working in this same area with another round of the cycle with the preservice teacher taking the lead role. A second option is to return to the observation cycle. This is not unusual at all to move back and forth between observations and lead teaching. The preservice teacher comes to the observation with a new set of eyes and questions. It is quite powerful. The third option is to move into a new area of teaching focus in a new activity structure. We offer a representation of these possible moves between observation and lead teacher in Figure 7.2.

The second part of the action plan is to list the things that are going to be taken forward into practice. Now is the time to reach for the pencil or the laptop. You can record or the preservice teacher can record. Keep it simple. Try to avoid any comments like, "If you had the teaching to do over again, what would you do differently?" This is backward thinking and not nearly as helpful as thinking forward in creating an action plan. Two or three ideas will work just fine as a place to start. Exchange copies of the action plan. This action plan

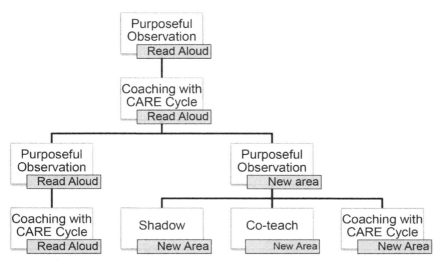

FIGURE 7.2 Next Steps After a CARE Coaching Cycle

moves you right into a planning phase. This is where your reflection becomes refraction—moving forward as a process that emerges because you've done the hard work of examining practice.

Most coaches find it useful to focus just a little part of the closing on the value of the cycle for the preservice teacher. It's an invitation to the preservice teacher to comment on the experience and help inform your growth. You are not asking for an evaluation—not, "Did this go well?" You are asking what parts of the experience were most helpful. You think about a couple of data sources: Who was talking most? How much did you actually have to draw on the road map or did the preservice teacher take the lead and get to the important work? How mechanical vs. "in flow" was the talk? In what ways did the conversation become dialogic? And, how does the action plan look as growth path?

The Planning Conference: Reflecting for Practice

Planning

Traditional approaches to planning tend to emphasize the movement from objectives (behavioral) into some kind of direct teaching structure (e.g., setting the stage; stating the objective; providing input; guided practice; checking for understanding; review and closure). Preservice teachers may have been prepared in this kind of model or in some other format that lends itself to the construction of written lesson plans in preparation to teach. Indeed, preservice teachers may have been introduced to multiple formats for lesson planning and it may be important to clarify as we move into practice. We must be very careful about aligning expectations around such areas as planning.

Several things stand out from research in teaching regarding planning. First, teachers plan carefully. Second, most experienced teachers do not use the kind of serial planning process represented in the traditional lesson plan. Third, the traditional lesson plan structure used most often does not fit with a lot of teaching activity (e.g., conferencing with students; guiding class meetings; support for problem-based learning). Experienced teachers tend to rely on routines for teaching where the content and focus may change but the structure is set. This is the work that was done in the previous chapter around Activity Configurations and Purposeful Observations. Your student should be approximating teaching in an area where they have an understanding of the basic activity structure, even if you have not shared a detailed Activity Configuration. It's a matter of them fitting the new content they will be supporting into the routine structure that they know.

There is a pretty standard argument that experienced teachers came through a detailed planning phase to get to the point that they don't need the level of planning they once needed. For this reason, it is likely a good idea that preservice teachers have a fairly developed plan for the teaching they will do. The written form of the plan (from fully scripted to just an outline) is more specific to the content or the process that is the focus for the teaching. The plan is a resource and a tool for the preservice teacher and you to use in supporting their teaching. The planning conference is less defined in space and time as the other three conferences in the CARE coaching cycle. You will sometimes find that the post-conference begins to shift over into a planning conference with a focus on the next. This is a very natural progression—just be sure that the reflecting on practice that is the focus in the post-conference has been mined for all it is worth.

One of the major markers of the shift into planning is the shift back into "we" discourse. Planning is collaborative and constructive. The cooperating teacher says, "It seems to me that many of the students are still struggling with the quick writes in response to read-alouds and it's mostly because of their concerns over spelling. This doesn't happen in turn and talks ... they are very active there. What can we do to reduce the apprehension around spelling?" This "we" discourse may be quite different from the reflective conversations that took place in the post-conference.

Teachers moving into the CARE model often ask questions like: "But when do I get to give them some ideas?" "When do I get to suggest some things they should be trying out?" "When do I get to be more direct in my coaching?" These are all valid questions when you consider the broad span that exists between a novice and an experienced teacher, and from the traditional understanding of what it means to coach. Coaching with CARE is different. Our first response to these kinds of questions is to remind the cooperating teachers that their work in modeling their practices, deconstructing these practices in the Activity Configurations, shadowing and co-teaching with the preservice teacher are very, very direct and explicit.

Our follow-up response is to suggest that the planning phase offers a lot of space for being direct in bringing in ideas for teaching in creating focus points for teaching growth that may have come out of an observation. It is not unusual at all for a cooperating teacher to see something in a teaching observation and decide: "This is something I want to attend to in planning. I'm not going to address it in the post-conference unless the preservice teacher brings it up." The example offered above regarding quick writes and the hesitation of the students around spelling could have been part of the post-conference but it could also be held out for planning where the teacher can (a) be more directive and (b) situate the work as problem-posing for us to do together. Another example, imagine a cooperating teacher who observes that the transitions in activity structures (e.g., moving from whole class into a small group activity with manipulatives) takes quite a bit of time. The preservice teacher does not bring this up. In the planning going forward the teacher might say, "It seems that there is a lot of difficulty in our class in moving between whole class and small group work. What's going on? Do you think it might help if we...?"

Planning is a time where we may reach out to other resources together. The cooperating teacher may have a book, or a chapter, or an article on a topic that might open up some ideas. The more the teacher can invite the preservice teacher into learning with her the more powerful the growth for everyone. The more the preservice teacher becomes invested in this part of the process, the easier it is to move out of the evaluative and into learning together—with all the bumps along the way. The most powerful statements in the action plan are the ones that lead to this kind of collaborative thinking and work.

A Case: Post-conference and Planning

We met Helen and Renee in Chapter 6, and now we will continue with them on their journey through the CARE cycle, focusing on the post-conference and subsequent planning phase. For this observation, Renee taught a mini-lesson on poetry and word work, as well as supported students as they read independently during reading workshop. Helen and Renee met the next day for the post-conference. We are providing an edited version of the post-conference transcript in order to highlight Helen's understandings of the post-conference structure and purpose. Similar to Jane and all of the cooperating teachers that we have had the privilege to work with over the years, you will see that Helen's language draws from Freire's five principles of humility, hope, faith, love, and critical thinking as she guides Renee and herself through reflecting on practice. Please notice the agency Renee enacts as an active participant in the post-conference and to the amount of space Renee takes for her talk. Again, we have emboldened phrases that Helen uses that reflect the coaching moves we expect to see in a post-conference.

> **Helen:** Let's talk a little bit about your lesson. **I want to hear what you are thinking about now.**
>
> **Renee:** I was a lot more comfortable mainly because we talked about it so much ahead of time. I still felt like I was losing the kids' engagement at certain points, and that was something that I have been reflecting on since then. I don't know how to regain that. I think a lot of them did come back to it on their own, but it felt like maybe there was something else I could have done to re-engage some of the kids.
>
> **Helen:** What I noticed was that you were actually engaging the kids and then you kept actually checking in with them. At times they might have lost focus a little bit, but they always came right back. **I gathered some data about** how you supported students if they were losing focus. I noticed that you checked in with the students, and you asked them if they were interested in working with a partner. That was another way you helped them to regain their focus.

Renee: Actually, the hardest thing that I realized for the first time is that when we get to independent reading time, that's when I have so much more ability to help them regain focus. But when I am up there, and it is the whole group, and they are not facing me because they are facing the projector, I realized it is more difficult to keep them engaged.

Helen: Ah! That makes a lot of sense. Let's talk about what you noticed during the lesson, and we can talk about this again at the end. **We will consider your realization as we create our action plan for your teaching next time. I am going to write that down, so we do not forget your thinking. When did you feel a flow in your lesson? What went really well?**

Renee: It was really fun to reread the poem in different voices. I really enjoyed having the kids come up with the voices.

Helen: Name some of your gems that you did during the lesson.

Renee: Like you said, trying to partner them up during independent reading. I felt like that was actually a good move. At first, I was thinking I will let them do that on their own, if they need that support, and then I kind of realized in the moment that the kids that need that support may not initiate it. I felt like that was a good move, "Hey, do you want to partner up with the person next to you?"

Helen: Absolutely. I felt like that really helped the students that needed that support and also regain focus for some of the students that needed to regain focus. **You asked me to focus on Kate and Evan during the lesson.** A few things that I noticed during the activity was that there were times when Kate was totally engaged and focused on what you were all doing. There was a moment where she did lose focus, but you immediately asked her if she could work with the person next to her. In regards to Evan, I noticed that he would sometimes lose focus and then come right back into it. You would do that sometimes by ignoring his behavior and allowing him to kind of come back naturally, which he did. Sometimes you supported him by checking in with him, and you also sat with him and asked him to work with a partner. I feel like the support you provided for both of them helped them to get back into the activity with everybody else. **You anticipated that there was going to be struggle with the part that focused on the long /i/ sound and the word "slobbering." What did you notice and what did you change?**

Renee: I thought that probably wasn't a word [slobbered] the kids would be that familiar with, but everyone seemed to have a solid understanding of what it meant. They also understood the long /i/ sound better than

I expected. What really surprised me was that they struggled with the rhyming words.

Helen: Yeah, that was really surprising.

Renee: It was weird. I thought they would easily recognize these rhyming words.

Helen: You stopped for a second with the poem, and you went into a conversation about rhyming words, so that was its own little focus lesson within the poetry activity. **Since there were some changes in the struggles that you noticed, what adjustments did you make in your lesson?**

Renee: I decided to cut the word work short because I spent time focusing on the rhyming words.

Helen: You made some different choices in the activity that you thought would accommodate their needs a little bit better based on what you noticed.

Renee: And I didn't want to lose their engagement. Since we talked about rhyming for a little bit longer I thought if we kept talking about the words they might become disengaged.

Helen: Yes. **Thinking about your focus on the rhyming words and also reflecting back on what we talked about earlier on some adjustments that you might want to make for next time, what do you want to try out in our next activity?**

Renee: I think it would be really beneficial to the students to spend a lot of time just focusing on rhyming, and I think doing the partner reading was really effective for a lot of them.

Helen: And you also mentioned something about positioning yourself differently because there was a challenge when you were sitting behind the kids at the projector. And it was easier to gain their focus when you could face them. **Thinking about your positioning, what do you think we can do to support them and support you?**

Renee: Well, I think instead of sitting at the projector and pointing on the projector, I could stand up in front of the class and point with the giant pointer. I think that would keep their focus of me being up there and work with the projection on the screen.

Helen: That makes me think that we can do some adjusting together to help because I want to try these adjustments too. I notice the same kind of challenges when I am working on poetry too because when you are behind them and it is kind of harder

to get their attention. We can find a way that we can adjust this lesson together in our next planning time, and we can find a way that we can do all of the things that you were just talking about. I really enjoyed watching your lesson today. And the kids also seemed really engaged and excited.

Renee: It was exciting. I am excited!

Helen: I am excited to keep trying and keep working.

Helen opened the post-conference with "I want to hear what you are thinking about now" in order to invite Renee as the primary narrator in the post conference. Early in the post-conference, Renee expressed her surprise at the challenges she felt maintaining student engagement when in whole group versus the ease she felt when she was able to meet with students individually. Often the feeling of surprise is accompanied with anxiety and tension, which can lead the preservice teacher to evaluate her or his performance, rather than reflect on practice.

Helen supported Renee in this moment of surprise. First, Helen reassured Renee that the students were engaged, "What I noticed was that you were actually engaging the kids and then you kept actually checking in with them." Next, Helen became more specific, drawing on data that Renee had asked her to collect to provide specific moves Renee made to support student engagement. And then, Helen made Renee's surprise important, by writing it down, and proposed the idea that they should both return to it at the end of the post-conference in their action plan as they move forward in teaching. And finally, Helen explicitly shifted the focus of the conversation to appreciation and asked Renee to share "what went really well" and "name some of your gems." Helen and Renee knew that they would have time at the end of the post-conference to consider the position of the teacher during a whole group lesson, and by saving further discussion for the end, Helen knew that they could bring this surprise forward into the productive space of planning and reflecting for practice.

Helen repeats this process of moving from Renee's thinking, to data, to making it important, to shifting to the next, appreciative topic throughout the post-conference. This structure is supportive of Renee, and both seem to know what will happen next and Renee is continuously positioned as the one doing the hard work of the teaching. In the end, Helen positions them as co-teachers who are learning about teaching poetry together, the content, and addressing the concerns of engagement and the teacher's placement in the room.

What comes out of the post-conference was a clear directive and action plan about the work is going forward, providing the basis for the next phase of the model, planning. Helen described her process for planning as a three-part process.

1. I explain the standards for first grade, standards for next grade (in order to prepare our students for next year), the developmental level of first graders, what challenges to expect, etc. We break down the sequence (that I have used in the past) for teaching a topic. We question the sequence and reflect forward.
2. After a couple days of her letting the ideas "cook," I then start to break down how she is going to teach the activities and think through what questions she still has regarding logistics of the lessons. I call this the logistics part of planning, and in this part, I provide a great deal of directive guidance for Renee. However, the lesson plan is co-constructed, with each person bringing ideas, evaluating those ideas, and voicing concerns and potential challenges. In this part of planning, I use the reflective model, privileging co-construction.
3. We fine-tune the lessons based on what we've already noticed the students struggle with/are successful with. We discuss how to support students. We address any areas of discomfort Renee may have (generally based on previous lessons). In this segment, I often model the language I would use when talking with students about an idea.

Helen's work is always to think about what comes out of the post-conference when preparing for the next phase, and often the third phase of planning and the pre-conference seem like they are seamless and continuous. However, the role she takes is different—she moves from co-construction to being a careful listener with the right questions to prompt Renee's lesson image.

Some Thinking and Talking To Do

*   The idea of a "road map" is one you might be able to pull apart a bit more in your thinking. When you look at a map for directions, there is quite a bit of filtering you do to locate where you are and how you'll get where you're going. For example, the app on your smartphone might take into consideration traffic, driving times, and even alternative pathways you can take en route. What might be filters you draw on as you're thinking about your road map for the post-conference?
*   Often, cooperating teachers worry that coaching with CARE prohibits them from "telling" or guiding the preservice teacher directly. What is the place of "telling" or directive coaching in the CARE model? Why might it be important to refrain from "telling" in the post-conference, in particular?
*   What are some ways that you might apply the notion of reflection turning into refraction, or constructing action plans to move into planning, in your own teaching? How might you keep up and keep track of how these action plans guide your practice?

Reference

Costa, A. L. and Garmston, R. J. (1994). *Cognitive coaching: A foundation for renaissance schools.* Norwood, MA: Christopher-Gordon Publishers.

PART III

The Three C's of CARE

Community, Critical, and Content

8

CLASSROOM COMMUNITIES AND CRITICAL SOCIAL ISSUES

Making peace is hard, hard, hard, but that's the price we must learn to pay for living on this planet.

(Mary Cowhey, author of *Black Ants and Buddhists*)

This chapter is the first of two that will address the three C's of CARE: Community, Critical and Content. The three C's are so important in the CARE model because they represent what you will be talking about in the coaching conversations within CARE. The three C's are the *what* but also the *so what* of CARE, in other words. This chapter will address the first two C's: Community and Critical, and we will return to the third C, Content, in Chapter 9.

In one of our favorite research studies on coaching and mentoring, Bieler (2010), a researcher who studied dialogue between a preservice teacher and mentor asked, "How can we create teacher preparation experiences that provide better opportunities for new teachers to 'feel their own strength,' to begin their careers with strong senses of themselves as actors and knowers?" (p. 392). Our work has been to disrupt traditional directive models of coaching and mentoring present throughout the literature. In this kind of model, a preservice teacher has few opportunities to develop critical or self-reflective practices because the mentor is positioned as powerful through her use of praise, approval, and correction. In this chapter, we will provide you with models and language to talk about power and a teacher's role in the classroom, as well as tools for addressing the issues of race, class, gender, and other critical social issues that are such an important part of teaching.

The First C in CARE: Classroom Communities

In other parts of this book, we have talked about the community of coaches you may be a part of and the practices of that community, in terms of how you might learn together about your coaching. However, in this chapter, we will address the topic of classroom communities. In our teacher preparation program, and in many programs throughout the country, preservice teachers take a course called Classroom Organization and Management. The idea of management in teaching is an old idea, part of the traditional and behaviorist views of teaching we discussed in Chapter 3. We have reframed this course to address the concerns that preservice teachers often have about their teaching. In our work, and your work with your preservice teacher, old frames will have to be examined and disrupted. This chapter is about that disruption. What should the work be about?

The work in coaching should emerge from two places—the preservice teacher's reflection on practice and your roadmap for the conferences. In this section, we briefly discuss the concerns that might come up in your use of the Coaching with CARE cycle and how those concerns might shift as part of your work together.

Concerns Theory

Concerns theory grew out of Francis Fuller's (1974) examination of the concerns of preservice teachers as they move through teacher preparation programs. When asked to express their concerns, she found that concerns were around two broad areas: concerns unrelated to teaching (e.g., the football team, personal relationships) and concerns related to teaching. Fuller (1974) focused her analysis on the concerns related to teaching and found that these fell into one of three categories:

> **Personal concerns.** These are concerns that focus on the preservice teacher. How am I doing? Am I meant to teach? Am I going to pass? Am I going to get a job?
>
> **Task concerns.** These are concerns that focus on the doing of teaching. How do I get the students to behave properly? How do I organize the morning schedule? How do I manage the movement into specials?
>
> **Impact concerns.** These are concerns focused on the impact of their teaching on students. Am I doing the best I can to promote community? How can I promote more powerful writing? How can the students pursue their own inquiry?

Addressing Concerns in Coaching

Concerns are to be expected as part of the change process. All of the concerns will be present at all times. You won't always be reframing conversations about management as community-building conversations. What Fuller (1974) did discover is that there is general progression in the relative intensity of concerns that moves from the personal to task to impact. The guiding principle in working with concerns is to make sure that the concerns at lover levels are addressed as much as possible. Movement toward other stages will come with time and support.

It can be easy to feel compelled to address all of the preservice teacher's concerns during a post-conference or planning conference, but we urge you to think about other times when you can address these concerns. Each of these concerns is and will become part of the pedagogical content knowledge (Shulman, 1986) that preservice teachers will construct as they engage in practice. We return to this idea in the next chapter.

Assessing concerns can be quite informal. Every few weeks or so, simply ask the preservice teacher jot down three things that are concerning them most. It's fairly easy to see the intensity and the stages of concern and this can lead to very productive conversations and actions to lower concerns that need to be addressed. This is an excellent exercise to do in collaboration with the field supervisor. The openness and joint work addressing concerns is helpful in building relationships and constructing a community of practice.

One of the first areas of concerns that we see and hear preservice teachers focus on in their talk is classroom management. For the preservice teacher, felt needs are often highest in this area. In part, at least at the preservice level, these needs are associated with the perception of no authority. "I'm not the real teacher in the classroom and the students won't do what I want them to do. How can I ever get control without being the teacher?" Authority, in traditional terms, is the key to a working classroom. Philip Jackson (1968) framed this perspective on the classrooms around issues of "crowds, praise, and power." Speaking of the hidden curriculum of schooling, he argued that schools are crowded places in which order is created and maintained through praise of good behavior and control of that which is less preferred, and that being in classrooms depends on one's acceptance and compliance with the difference in authority between teacher and student. We know these concerns are real and that the authority perspective is dominant in the discourse of teaching, but we are going to problem pose in a different way than is traditional. We begin by deconstructing the concept of management as something that is necessary in teaching.

One problem with traditional notions of classroom management is that academics are treated as something separate from management but in reality these two are closely connected. In a classroom that is struggling to learn (in the healthy sense of struggle), challenges will surface and will sometimes test levels of cooperation among classroom members or between learners and teachers. The more risk and the more ambiguity in the curriculum the more likely it is that work will become more active (e.g., noise levels, movement, participation, disruption) and the greater the need for differentiated support from the teacher. The less risk and less ambiguity in the work of the classroom the more likely you will see high levels of compliance. The management solution is sometimes found in reducing the challenges of work to achieve cooperation and compliance. The problem with this solution is that learning is diminished, agency is diminished, and motivation is diminished. The preservice teacher needs to learn to value work in the classroom that promotes growth and expect that challenges in participation are going to come with the territory of the often risky and sometimes uncertain condition of meaningful learning.

A second problem with traditional conceptions of management is that the tools of control are rooted in behaviorist traditions. Manipulating rewards and punishment are keys to the well-managed classroom. The teacher must assert her authority and shape students toward compliance. Many teachers believe that when order is in place, the real teaching begins, and without such order, nothing can be taught and learned in schools.

Our approach is to recast the challenge in classrooms from implementing order to building a classroom community of learners—inclusive of teachers and students. We want to reframe notions of authority (and accountability) as responsibility to each other. This shift will require a careful examination of the words we use to describe what we are doing. We will need to become bilingual in the sense that students come into our class with certain expectations for how classrooms work based on their history and we have to teach them a second language that connects what they expect with what they will be experiencing. The same is true in communicating with other teachers and administrators. The reflective process of CARE: from Purposeful Observations, to shadowing and co-teaching, to engaging in the CARE conference cycle is the pathway to address these issues of classroom community, as opposed to classroom management. What follows is a set of aspects of building a classroom community. These might inspire you to write an Activity Configuration or engage in a Purposeful Observation with your preservice teacher, as a way to reframe questions of control and management as community conversations.

Aspects of Building a Classroom Community

Community Agreements

When we make agreements, we articulate "who we are" and "why we are here," as well as differences and strength in diversity. We talk about different roles and different kinds of responsibilities. We talk about how we want our classroom to look, to feel and to sound like. See Figure 8.1 for an example of a community agreement.

This use of agreements is central in social emotional learning curricula and in TRIBES (Gibbs, 1994) or social emotional learning curricula. These are programs that take steps to build the character qualities and strategies that are useful in building a democratic and caring classroom. It may be useful to explore with the preservice teacher some of the core dimensions of building a community

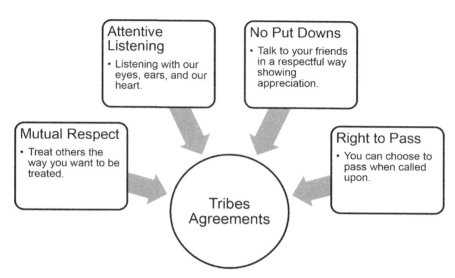

FIGURE 8.1 Classroom Agreements Adapted from TRIBES (Gibbs, 1994)

of learners, such as trust, identity, cooperation, predictability, respect, choice, friendship, sense of humor, and problem-solving. This listing is not exhaustive of areas of importance but it is a good place to start, in particular with attention to setting up the classroom at the start of the year and the first weeks of school where community building is such a strong focus.

Transitions

In classroom life, we move from topic to topic, from one activity to another. Sometimes these transitions mark a shift in our mental focus. Sometimes these transitions involve physical movement and shifts in the ways we participate in the work. The students in the classroom may not know exactly when (or why) these shifts are going to happen. They may be engaged in completing some other task. How do you alert them to a change that is coming up? How do you close down one kind of work and move into another? What is the expectation for time in the transition? What will it be like when we get to our new space? The building of routines will help simplify over time, but initially these kinds of things need to be attended to explicitly through explanations and reminders (e.g., who we are, how we work together). Some teachers may like to play soft music during major transitions.

Overlappingness

This is a term derived from the work of Jacob Kounin (1970) and refers to the fact that elementary classrooms are busy and complicated spaces. There often are multiple activities going on at the same time. Some of the activities may be with a teacher and some may not. Some students may be engaged in small-group project work while some of the students may be working independently. There is a common pattern among new teachers to become so engaged in the work they are doing with a small group or a conference with an individual student that they lose contact with what the rest of the class is doing. There are some important strategies and moves the teacher can make to ensure that there is full engagement with the students in front of her but awareness as well of what all the other students are doing. It can be as simple as a visual sweep of the classroom every minute. It can be comments (appreciations) toward the work of individuals or small groups working in other areas of the room. Teachers do not, as according to some lore, have eyes in the backs of their heads. They position themselves in ways that keep them aware of how the community is working at all times.

"Withitness"

This term also comes out of the work of Jacob Kounin (1970) and refers to the teacher's awareness of what is going on in the classroom (as with overlappingness) but focuses more on what to ignore, what to attend to, and when. There are two major dimensions to "withitness" that have been gathered from watching teachers build and sustain a working community. The first is that the teacher is very aware of where something started. So often, it's the next student responding down the line that gets noticed. This is not the case of establishing fault or blame but rather understanding all the complexity of situations. The second dimension of "withitness" is knowing what to ignore (i.e., leaving the students to resolve issues using the strategies you have been promoting in class). If the teacher does determine to get involved, then this occurs before there is escalation or spread (involving additional students). Proximity is a first step (moving closer if possible). There is no simple formula for responding but understanding the range of choices available is very important.

Using Signals

Some classes may agree on a simple signal for a self-check on working within agreements. This may be a soft bell sound or a chime. In cases where the teacher might want to have the attention of the entire class there may be a simple saying that the teacher says and the students complete. All of these strategies should be part of the agreement-building process.

Attention Spans

Sometimes we just exhaust ourselves with work. Every once in awhile we might need a "brain break" or a shift in the activity. Recognizing the signs of needing a break is a good first step.

Source Focus

In small group and whole class work, students are sometimes confused about where to focus their attention. Generally, when students are clear on the focus point the flow works a little better. We have seen this in particular in the use of media in the classroom. Something is being projected from the back to the front of the room. The students are sitting in a group facing the screen. The teacher is behind the projector and managing the images. The teacher is trying to engage the students in a conversation but where is the focus? Who are they talking with? The screen? The teachers? The other students? Think about the ways in which these complicated settings can be arranged to keep the focus points as clear and natural as possible.

Making Work Visible

Classrooms are filled with work. This work may be intellectual or aesthetic and observable. One useful strategy in classroom work is to ensure there are products associated with the work. These products can be observed in process or as artifacts after the work is completed. A discussion of a text is visible in the moment but adding a product expectation to the work (e.g., a list of points made, questions raised) is very useful for both the teachers and the students to reflect on. There is the cognitive bonus of transmediation as meaning is constructed across different language or sign systems. There is the additional benefit of enriching the text environment of the classroom with local texts. The product is not the goal for the work but the product does reveal, in its construction and presentation, insights into growth.

Space, Aesthetics, and Flow

Think carefully about each space in the classroom and the expectations for the kind of work that will be completed in that space. Think about flow and movement in the classroom. Think about the teacher's perspective from all angles. Think about the aesthetic dimensions of the classroom—the colors, the images, and sounds. Attention to these factors can help promote a sense of community and belonging.

As you engage with your preservice teacher around these processes, you may find yourself challenged in your own practices. This is the kind of space where a mentor becomes most powerful. You show curiosity. You show vulnerability. You take risks. This is the kind of mentor a preservice teacher needs most. You can grow together.

The Second C in CARE: Critical Coaching

Now we move to the second C, critical. As part of our research on the CARE model, we have been considering the different meanings of critical in CARE. In Chapter 11 on RCA, we will discuss the frame of "disruptive" in relation to video-focused coaching, about moments of surprise and challenge. This is one meaning of the word "critical"—the work to disrupt the commonplace (Lewison et al., 2002) or ask, "Why is it that way? What other ways could it be?" When we engage in CARE, we are always workinsg in this way. Our use of Activity Configurations allows us a window into practices, and as we know more about our practices, we can begin to ask these hard questions. It is through CARE that we are able to problem-pose and solve around those practices, and through the practice, begin to feel how powerful our teaching and reflection can become.

One of our teachers, Helen, who we introduced in earlier chapters, chose to follow Renee, the preservice teacher's, lead and address disruptive moments in their CARE cycles. Her first foray was engaging her preservice teacher around sharing time—a time in her first grade classrooms when students got to tell stories about their lives. Like others who have studied this part of the school day, Helen was asking questions about purposes and goals in terms of whose narrative styles were recognized and whose were deemed unfit for the sharing time space (see Michaels, 1981). Renee engaged in this work by reflecting on how much work she was doing, as a teacher, when it was the student's turn to tell his story. Later in the semester, Renee revisited questions of her own power and position in the classroom, reflecting after watching a video of her teaching in which she had been focusing on not touching students' materials, giving students "more power in the situation." She provided an example of two students who were confused about an image that appeared to show eight different moons in the sky. While she could have easily stepped in and explained that the picture was showing different phases of the same moon, she gave them space to figure it out. Subsequently, the students surprised her by using another text as a resource to support their inquiry and discovered "the illustrator put eight moons to show us the different sides to see."

These examples illustrate how preservice teachers can come to explore disruptive moments in teaching. However, there is a second meaning of critical in CARE. Drawing from critical pedagogy and theory, we also mean that preservice and cooperating teachers may need a framework for thinking about critical social issues in their teaching. Critical social issues have always been central in our work with teachers because our program has a mission to prepare teachers to work in culturally and linguistically diverse settings, and in those settings, we often see inequities in terms of what kinds of educational practices, materials, and resources those schools offer their students. Critical moments in teaching often come about because there are conflicts between what we intend to teach and what we are asked to teach, especially in a high-stakes testing era.

We would like to emphasize that each time we address a critical social issue in coaching, we are forging new ground and must be brave explorers. We may have to admit how little we know and what we are unable to do in the classroom, and that is a vulnerable position to take. In our work, however, we have seen that it is worth it. We teach our preservice teachers that they can be vulnerable too, and we open spaces for everyone to think more deeply about the world we are making for our students.

Another pair with whom we worked, Francine and Colleen, brought up the critical issue of racism in their coaching conversations. Like Renee, Colleen chose a moment as disruptive while watching a video of a classroom interaction. Colleen opened the conversation by pointing out a student's distracting behavior. Francine shifted the conversation, noting that he was the only African-American boy in the class. Francine spoke, while Colleen expressed her agreement:

> Yeah. I think that for us to be aware, first of all, you know, like I do notice, like just to put myself really, really out there, like I do notice sometimes with him, like, I do feel this greater sense of control.... Like one day he was eating fruit roll-ups in here. And I asked him to spit it out. And he didn't. And I really had to watch myself in that moment because that really upset me. But, that was a disproportionate amount of upsetness that I felt.

Francine talked about her own struggle to think through how her expectations for behavior are linked to whiteness, a racial position as well as a theory of the ways that racism operates through the actions and discourse of society. Francine modeled for Colleen how she was thinking about her response to students when they were bending the rules in class, and encountered her own racism through reflection right in front of her preservice teacher. We have seen pairs address issues of gender and language in the classroom, and also seen teachers plan units together about language ideology and why some languages are valued and others erased in schools. The possibilities are endless, but the word is never easy. One struggle you'll definitely encounter is finding the right balance between modeling your critical thinking in a space where the preservice teacher must take the lead. You'll want to look for that shared focus and attention that allows these issues to be co-constructed and powerful moving forward.

In order to make this work effective, cooperating teachers, preservice teachers, and university field supervisors will have to form learning communities that provide space for purposeful, open, and rich discussions and shared learning. All members of the learning community will need to understand that the conditions for the development of a supportive learning community that allowed for reflective mentoring to take place.

A Case: Disruptions in Teaching

Jane, a mentor we introduced in an earlier chapter, taught us much about how important critical social issues can be to mentoring and coaching. Jane was a veteran teacher, who identified as white, who had worked in both very linguistically and culturally diverse communities in the past but was currently working in a school in which there was less diversity and most students' families had lots of resources and experienced cultural alignment with school practices. As a way to explore issues of community, culture, and critical issues with Jane's cohort of cooperating teachers, we asked them to write three essays. The first was a historical look at becoming a teacher; the second a mentor. The third was a critical teacher autobiography, in which teachers explored their process of "becoming" a critical teacher. In this autobiography, Jane let us know that race was becoming salient in her classroom context, as one of her students, who was African American, was participating differently in classroom conversations than his peers, and the ways he was interacting were leading her and her preservice teacher to have lots of conversations about race, language, and power in the classroom.

Stephanie, the preservice teacher in Jane's classroom, was also African American. About four months into their work together, Jane used a coaching cycle to explore issues of race, diversity, and equity with Stephanie. The coaching cycle centered around a writing mini-lesson conducted by Stephanie. Initially, the coaching cycle focused on Stephanie's reflective and responsive teaching. Towards the end of the post-conference Jane brought up turn-taking in the whole group discussion and the differences between Chance's style of discourse and that of his peers.

There is a critical moment in this conference as well. One student, Chance, who is African American, contributed long turns to the lesson. Jane wondered,

> His style of discourse is very (short pause), he tells a story, right? […] How can you balance talk? Because we want to give Chance a lot of time to practice, but at the same time, how can you encourage others to talk?

Here, Jane poses a collaborative challenge, one that they can address together. She was working simultaneously to address both a disruptive moment, one that challenged her as a teacher, but also to address a larger critical social issue. That social issue was the mismatch between narratives that teachers expect during sharing or community circle time and the narrative styles of speakers of African-American English. Sarah Michael's work on sharing time was informing her question, and she was identifying Chance's "topic-centered" way of interacting with the style that Michaels identified in her analysis of sharing time.

Jane was studying classroom discourse analysis and frameworks that suggest multiple interactional styles in the classroom as part of her graduate coursework, and Stephanie was discovering herself as a workshop teacher and mastering language about instruction and students. In her response, Stephanie reframed the question, focusing on providing opportunities for all students to share. In doing so, she takes up the identity of workshop teacher, suggesting a "mini-lesson," different ways for students to engage (e.g., "turn and talks"), and thinking about how to perhaps further their workshop goals of understanding the work of authors for the students.

Together, Jane and Stephanie co-constructed a critical social issue to bring to the students—the idea of multiple styles of discourse. Here, the focus was not on encouraging students to "build tolerance" towards Chance's style, but to "validate his way of thinking." She then turned her focus to Chance, positioning herself as someone who understands his style of discourse ("I can see where he's going with it"); again, perhaps this was because she is also African American. She then moved the conversation away from a discussion of different styles of discourse, and the questions of race and culture that accompany this discussion, back towards the curriculum ("to practice those retelling skills, kind of hitting those important details to help him kind of make his point").

What have learned from this case and others is that you can enact the CARE model without ever addressing critical social issues in your teaching. Questions about language, access, and race might always stay in the periphery. Responsive/reflective mentoring can center on "safe" issues: curriculum, instruction, responsive teaching; however, our classrooms are sociocultural spaces in which larger issues shape our decisions about teaching. We need tools to address these issues, however, and the cooperating teachers we have worked with have continuously put themselves out there—making space for those conversations with their preservice teachers.

Some Thinking and Talking To Do

- I didn't know this book was going to be about classroom management. Do I really have to organize and manage my classroom in a particular way to use the Coaching with CARE model? This all seems pretty complicated and unnecessary.
- How do you imagine addressing the "critical" in your coaching? Can you imagine addressing larger issues we have not talked about, such as the effects of high stakes testing on students of color, or the under-resourcing of schools in communities that experience poverty?
- In this chapter we write about assessing concerns of your preservice teacher and becoming responsive. The research on concerns theory has expanded over the years. The research has revealed that it is not unusual, in times of change or adoption of a particular practice, for people to move through different levels of intensity of concerns (self, task, and impact). How is this true of you in moving into the coaching with CARE? What are your top three concerns right now as you move into this community of practice?

References

Bieler, D. (2010). Dialogic praxis in teacher preparation: A discourse analysis of mentoring talk. *English Education*, *42*(4), 391–426.

Fuller, F. F. (1974). A conceptual framework for a personalized teacher education program. *Theory into Practice*, *13*(2), 112–122.

Gibbs, J. (1994). *TRIBES: A new way of learning together*. Santa Rosa, CA: Center Source Publications.

Jackson, P. W. (1968). *Life in classrooms*. New York, NY: Holt, Rinehart, and Winston.

Kounin, J. S. (1970). *Discipline and group management in classrooms*. New York: Holt, Rinehart, and Winston.

Lewison, M., Flint, A. S., and Van Sluys, K. (2002). Taking on critical literacy: The journey of newcomers and novices. *Language arts*, 79(5), 382–392.

Michaels, S. (1981). "Sharing time": Children's narrative styles and differential access to literacy. *Language in Society*, 10(3), 423–442.

Shulman, L. S. (1986). Those who understand: Knowledge growth in teaching. *Educational Researcher*, 15(2), 4–14.

9

CONTENT MATTERS

There are many ways of going forward, but only one way of standing still.
(Franklin D. Roosevelt)

In this chapter, we will explore the third C in CARE—content, because a focus on content will move us forward in our teaching. There is a myth around the coaching of teachers (preservice and beyond): "If you know the basics of coaching, the content probably doesn't matter." While there are many themes that we have come back to again and again in our writing about the coaching with CARE model (e.g., the importance of reflection, the relationships, practice, challenge, community, a critical stance), we do not believe that the techniques of coaching exist independent of content. Content matters. We believe that the place where disciplinary knowledge intersects with pedagogical knowledge—what Shulman (1986) called "pedagogical content knowledge"—is fundamental to quality teaching and therefore to quality coaching.

First, let's talk about content knowledge. If you teach at the elementary level, you may find that you have deep content knowledge in some areas, and that in other areas, your knowledge is just beginning to develop. As secondary content area teachers, you might find your content knowledge is much deeper—perhaps you have a deep passion for Tejano history or a strong content base in algebra and geometry. No matter what level, however, teachers find themselves learning alongside their students, and at other times will feel they have expertise in a subject.

Shulman (1986) differentiated between content knowledge and pedagogical content knowledge (PCK)—the methods of inquiry and teaching that are associated with a certain discipline. PCK includes the following dimensions:

- The topics that are taught in a content area and "the most useful forms of representation of those ideas, the most powerful analogies, illustrations, examples, explanations, and demonstrations" (p. 9);
- What makes learning in this area easy or challenging for students, in particular students with different background experiences or learning histories; and
- In many areas, the particular puzzles, key questions, and misconceptions that students might encounter in a particular content area or topic.

In addition to knowledge that teachers hold from teaching in a particular area, PCK can also be seen as a reflection of the ways that experts learn about the world through different established methods of inquiry. Some of these systems of inquiry (e.g., the "scientific method"; use of "primary documents" by a historian) have been formalized while other systems are evolving. Botanists pursue questions and apply tools of inquiry that are unique within their scientific community and particular to their content. Anthropologists pursue questions and have tools of inquiry that are particular to their domain. Teaching around these areas involves more than just surveying the findings from these disciplines. Teaching around these disciplines must include the examination of and experiences with the tools a discipline uses to gather and interpret data. Engagement with these processes of what, why, and how we study the world around us is as much a part of an early childhood curriculum as it is part of graduate study.

The idea of content knowledge and PCK are challenges for elementary educators who teach across subjects throughout the day in ways that secondary educators may not experience. For example, we might wonder *how deep* teachers' content knowledge ought to be in order to teach across subjects. In Texas, where we prepare teachers, the state recently revised a certification exam called the Core Subjects EC-6 Exam to be much more challenging in terms of content domains, causing us to look again at our program and undergraduate education to find out how we are preparing teachers for the level of specificity they need to know in order to be certified to teach in our state.

In introducing these ideas around content, we are not suggesting that the curriculum at the elementary level (or any other level for that matter) should be divided along disciplinary lines. What we are suggesting is that knowing how scientists within a discipline engage in their work is important to learning in that domain, and that content is always growing and shifting. We also believe that practices of reading and writing should be integrated into inquiry across disciplines.

In this chapter, we will address the idea that content and PCK matter when we are engaging in disciplinary work as coaches. Our focus on content has grown out of our observation of cooperating teachers working with preservice teachers across different content areas, particularly in areas that introduce challenges in terms of content knowledge and PCK. We have concluded that coaches who have a strong disciplinary perspective display greater flexibility in their coaching in the planning phase in particular but in post-conferencing as well. These coaches seem less textbook-bound in their planning ("What's the next thing to cover in the grade level standards?") and less bound in their thinking to the procedural routines around teaching ("In a writers' workshop you must do ...").

In constructing this chapter, we have reached out to dialogue with experts in teacher education who have a disciplinary focus to describe how the understanding of their discipline might be important in teaching and coaching. We asked our experts to consider traditional representations of the curriculum in their discipline (as represented in the Common Core) and then to talk about innovative or alternative perspectives that might reveal some disciplinary complexity not revealed in the traditional curriculum. We will cover mathematics, writing, science, and reading; not a comprehensive list but the areas where elementary teachers' attention are most focused.

Teaching and Coaching in Mathematics

Dr. Susan Empson, The University of Missouri at Columbia

Of all the discipline areas we have worked with in teacher preparation, mathematics rises to the top as a concern for both preservice and cooperating teachers. Often these concerns are expressed in the form of a fear or a loathing of the subject. Sometimes this stance is rooted in a low estimate of their own capabilities and sometimes in their experiences as a student in classrooms. In many cases this means that teachers tend to rely heavily on the plans and procedures laid out in adopted textbooks. With limited confidence in their own abilities, they find it difficult to stray from the path laid out for them by those seen as experts and therefore less likely to be responsive to students with the adaptations made in the moment. Mathematics can be a difficult area for coaching, because these affective difficulties and limited understandings may be present for the cooperating teacher as well. In methods courses, teacher educators sometimes struggle with the kinds of activities and approaches that will help student teachers move past some of these affective barriers and anxieties.

Teaching Mathematics: Professional Knowledge

Dr. Empson began by confirming that our claims regarding the uncertainties and insecurities around the teaching of mathematics have been widely confirmed in the research literature. She further confirmed that test-driven curriculum for mathematics and the teaching mathematical procedures were common in the field. These two aspects of mathematics education can make learning to teach a challenge. How do we begin to break away from these patterns of teaching at the surface level? How do we move from doing something the right way and quickly? How do we not fall into the trap of thinking that every little thing we teach must be mastered by students before we move to teach the next thing? There were several recurring themes that Dr. Empson brought up in her conversation with us: a focus on children's mathematical thinking, careful attention to tasks, the teacher as a dialogue facilitator, and the importance of tools in learning.

The students we teach know a lot about mathematics—even very young children. Our orientation in teaching should be centered on and revealing of what kids know and how they think. They will have to construct new understandings on top of what they bring. Dr. Empson suggests:

> The goal should be to see the world through kids' eyes. What does multiplication look like? Well maybe it looks like making groups of things at first. Curriculum can be helpful in seeing endpoints. What is important is to understand what the kids' movement toward these endpoints looks like. Understanding is not an all or nothing thing and if you really want to build understanding in math you need to begin with what the kid understands rather than what they don't understand.

If the teacher can start with a genuine curiosity for what kids are thinking, good things will come forward.

Being and becoming a mathematician is the goal of any mathematics curriculum. Dr. Empson emphasized that the work of a mathematics teacher is to imagine what students' thinking might look like at the endpoint, and then think about the work that the teacher and students will be doing to build those understandings. There is this growing standardization of instruction that follows a "gradual release of responsibility" path. "Watch me do" (the teacher modeling). "Now, let's do it together" (guided practice). "Now, you do it on your own" (independent practice). Dr. Empson sees the teaching of mathematics starting in and ending up in a very different place. She sees the role of the teacher as very different as well. She stresses the importance of creating tasks that are challenging to the learner—but not overwhelming, what Stein and Smith (2011) named as having the right level of cognitive demand. "Here the kids are taking responsibility from the start." These are not tasks that "ask a child to reproduce a procedure" but are tasks that are expansive and generative in their potential to stimulate thinking. She sees these tasks as strongly connected to the lives of the students in terms that are familiar in their lives. She sees these tasks as rich in possibilities for different solutions to come forth—all with merit. She sees the learners working together and individually to complete their work.

Dr. Empson suggests that the way into preparing teachers in mathematics is to start with working with kids. Kids will teach, she explains, so much about the development of mathematical thinking. When we talk to kids about what they are doing while solving a problem, the key is to be curious. To ask, "Why did you choose to move those blocks to this group?" When teachers ask these questions, they gain insight into kids' thinking, and when asking many students what they are working on, we can begin to see how kids are developing cognitive understandings. The teacher's role is to create dialogue in those moments that flow out of careful observation and just the right conversation starter at just the right moment (What are you trying out? Tell me more. Have you done this before? What else have you tried? What tools are you using?). These are what Dr. Empson refers to as "mathematical conversations." Dr. Empson feels that these simple conversations are a very safe place for a teacher to start reforming the way they think about mathematics. The teacher brings these small conversations and resulting ideas forward to the students as a class at the end to make sense of the various strategies they employed and how they can be useful moving forward.

Coaching around Mathematics

One of the coaching cases we have studied in depth was centered on a mathematics lesson taught by a preservice teacher. The lesson had been drawn from the teacher's guide for the mathematics textbook used in the district. The lesson went pretty much as planned. What stood out in the post conference was the procedural level of focus. There was an easy flow to the post conference with the preservice teacher taking much of the lead and the cooperating teacher affirming most everything that was said. All the right questions were posed. Data was shared. Action plans were developed. It could have very well been regarded as a model for a CARE cycle. With time and distance though we started questioning everything about the cycle. How did anyone grow in this experience? What were the struggles around? What kind of engagement was there? The more we rewatched the video of the experience the more we became convinced that we had all fallen short on our goals as teachers and teacher educators. We had taken something conceptually rich (teaching mathematical concepts) and turned it into something very procedural. We were fooling ourselves and perhaps our students as well.

We have been thinking about particular coaching moves that you might see within the planning, pre-conference, teaching, and post-conference within each content area. In mathematics, as in every area, each of these areas holds puzzles for us as coaches. Most preservice teachers will need you to plan alongside them for mathematics teaching, because mathematics pedagogy is challenging. The curriculum, under Common Core, may be quite different from what the teachers themselves experienced in their own education. And, the methods of teaching in mathematics that you value might also be outside of their experience.

Helen, who we introduced in Chapters 6 and 7, taught us that the mathematics curriculum was so conceptually rich that she felt that three planning meetings were necessary for each lesson: First, Helen explained the curriculum standards and different approaches she had used in the past to teach the concept of time to first graders within that standard; second, after a day had passed, they met again to discuss some of the ideas that the preservice teacher had generated for her own teaching; and finally, a day before the unit began, they met again to go over the preservice teacher's exact plans and problem-pose and problem-solve around the unit. Planning is a major component of the coaching process, and what Helen did here was to support her preservice teacher in the curriculum.

Another entry point to coaching in mathematics might not be through the planning of curriculum but might be through work with a student. Imagine a setting in which you, the cooperating teacher, work next to your preservice teacher and a student or students to collaboratively examine students' thinking. Perhaps the teachers are sitting side-by-side with a student, and one is leading the conversation with the child as the other observes. Perhaps the student teacher interviews students as they are working on a task posed by the cooperating teacher, bringing back data to share in the post-conference. Here, the focus of the coaching would be on the students, a collaborative inquiry into the dialogue around problems that supports student thinking. As you continue through the chapter, we will build on these two entry points into coaching in the content areas.

Teaching and Coaching in Writing

Dr. Randy Bomer, The University of Texas at Austin

Writing is a discipline area that often is less likely than reading or mathematics to come with a structured program; there are not that many kits or sets of materials for teachers to work with. Based on your own identity and history as a writer, you may feel like this is the time in your day when students are most engaged and creative! Or perhaps, you work within a school culture that values writing instruction that focuses more on structure and mechanics, and you find this way of teaching writing to be frustrating. Although it is one of the less defined or shaped areas of the curriculum across school contexts, writing is a part of the entire day of a classroom, and writing instruction intersects with the arts, every curricular area, and every grade level. And more than other areas, experts have argued that teachers of writing must be writers themselves; that in order to coach others around writing, you must be working on your own craft. This idea has brought teachers together in communities to think about their teaching of writing, such as the National Writing Project, which supports local centers in providing professional development for teachers in or out of schools. However, there are many puzzles that educators face about the teaching of writing, and those puzzles will also come into our coaching work.

Teaching Writing: Professional Knowledge

If you have been teaching and attending writing professional development, you might find that your own practice borrows from many sources, what we might consider the "professional knowledge" of teaching writing. Teaching is professional knowledge, as Dr. Bomer suggested to us in our conversations with him about writing, which can come from many sources. Teachers are often asked to "take what you will" from a workshop or professional development back to their classroom, and those tricks or practices become part of that professional knowledge. For example, you may have attended a workshop in which you learned a specific process for teaching workshop, the structure of a mini-lesson, or even specific mini-lessons that support students in writing across different genres. In one district where we work, we often see an anchor chart on the wall with a smattering of "Sparkle Words," words that add specificity or imagery to a piece of writing. Teachers' practices come from different sources, but practices also gain a life of their own as they travel across spaces and get taken up by communities of teachers. As these practices move and build momentum, they increasingly are seen as "best practices" and also become more powerful.

Mary Kennedy (1999), as cited by Dr. Bomer in our interview, has made the argument that teaching of writing traditionally focused on a set of rules and structures that can be applied across contexts. Students are taught to use grammatical forms as well as the structures of genre to communicate ideas. However, it is often not the ideas that matter to teachers, but adherence to the rules and structures of language. This approach to teaching writing misses the boat, because what students do not gain is an understanding of how writing is a form of thinking, how revision impacts the weight of the piece, how communication is facilitated by writing, and how writers improvise or bend the rules as part of their art.

Rather, teachers of writing might approach writing as an art, and in that model, the teacher's attention is on the object that is made and what it represents. This view of writing asks the teacher to appreciate the work of the student. Sometimes, the teacher might provide a prescription or model of a kind of writing, but at that point, the work is to find out what the student is doing with that prescription and to work alongside the "artist" on his or her craft. Bomer pointed out to us that when writing is an art, and not a structure to be taught, that the teacher has all sorts of new questions to think about in terms of his or her role in the classroom and the structure of the work space. Art has a specific audience, and in this view of writing, students are clear about audience when doing their work. When children write poems, produce plays, or make art, an additional purpose beyond learning the forms of the genres is to entertain, inspire, and make the world more rich and beautiful. Bomer reminded us that when students create art, they are just like a poet or playwright who makes their artwork in the world. People come to their art as a visitor and appreciate (or not) in the same ways.

Now that you've heard these two different approaches, where do you sit in your thinking about the teaching of writing? In what ways does your writing curriculum privilege structure and/or art, and in what ways have you taught writing that conflates these two approaches? In what ways do you think about writing?

It may be that you answer, "Well, it's both, of course! ... Right?" We agree that students will encounter both views of writing in their experiences of schools, and sometimes, they will be working in both dimensions at the same time. Returning to the notion of PCK, we might think then about the forms of teaching that correspond with each approach and both approaches. If your work is to help students to develop their craft and art, in what ways might you set up a classroom environment for writing? If your focus is on teaching structures and genres, what might those moments look like? Do you have places for writers to write alone and to share their work in groups? How much time do students spend on their writing, including drafting, revision, and editing, and do they do so alone or in groups? Who determines how writing is revised? How is writing shared and displayed in the room? How do students know when a piece of writing is finished? Who is the audience for the written work? Often writing teachers play with these questions across the year, moving in and out of different units of study.

Developing a pedagogical set of practices for teaching writing is not an easy task. As a classroom teacher you are working with a group of students, all who have different ways of doing the craft of writing. For a long time, schools have been designed around standards and it's very hard for to think about how to teach genre/topics and mechanics *and* support students in their craft. Teachers have to contend with the choice of a genre study format, in which students might have topic choice within work with a particular genre; or a workshop in which students have choice of genre but maybe are working with a content standard in their writing (e.g., the Civil War). Bomer reminds us that very little attention has been paid to what it means to ask a group of children to produce within a standards-based curriculum.

Coaching around Writing

Deepening our professional knowledge is hard work, and the work of teaching and coaching is to examine our practice. There are a few ways this happens in the teaching of writing. As a coach of writing instruction, we would encourage you first to think about your philosophies of writing instruction and the practices you currently employ in your teaching. What does writing instruction mean to you? What is the role of writing in your own personal and professional life, and how does your history as a writer shape your teaching? How will you share these ideas with your preservice teacher? As in other content areas, you might ask your preservice teacher to conduct Purposeful Observations of your teaching in writing and then help you to reflect on what you believe about the teaching of writing. Within conferring, or any complex practice, there is going to be explicit value in modeling, in asking the preservice to watch what I do. This is what Grossman et al. (2009) calls the representation of practice—much like using a video case. However, this is not all—we also want to be concerned with the deconstruction of such practices. Maybe you ask your preservice teacher to sit beside you when do you talk to a student about his writing, but the next time, you sit next to her as she approximates the practice. You may find it worthwhile to continue to rotate in these roles, sharing together the work of observing and reflecting on practice, and developing PCK around the teaching of writing, exploring how teachers talk to kids to elicit their thinking in writing.

Building on earlier discussions of coaching that is centered on the classroom activity structures for teaching writing, we might need to think about coaching within different activity systems. Your role as a coach might be different within the different structures of the writing classroom. For example, what would coaching look like when you are doing assessment (looking at student work with or without students for the purpose of understanding what students know)? What might coaching look like around the choice of topics for teaching (i.e., what to focus on in my mini-lesson, and how to deliver a mini-lesson to a class)? What might coaching look like when preservice teachers are learning to sit beside a child to talk about a piece of writing (what many call conferring?) It may be that across different parts of the writing curriculum, your coaching might look very different.

Teaching and Coaching in Social Studies

Dr. Cinthia Salinas, The University of Texas at Austin

The social studies include areas of history, economics, geography, and often studies of communities and democratic citizenship. In no other area might the question of content knowledge come into such clear focus. In order to teach the social studies, there is a strong sense in the educational community that teachers need to have both deep and broad knowledge in these areas in order to teach. In addition, as in every discipline, there are habits of inquiry in each of these areas that inform teachers' PCK—what some would call the methods of teaching the social studies. It is very clear, in the social studies as well as in other areas, that content and pedagogical content knowledge are very closely related. It is hard to think about a teacher knowing content in social studies (e.g., events leading up to the Holocaust, the importance of branches of government) without also knowing how experts come to understand more about historical events, systems, and communities.

Teaching Social Studies: Professional Knowledge

What is taught in the social studies? Dr. Salinas, who we interviewed to inform our writing of this chapter, argues that by in large, history is taught as the social studies, at the expense of teaching about economics, citizenship, or geography.

Again, standards play a large role in what teachers choose to teach in the social studies, and there are often battles in state legislatures and school districts about what will be included in the curriculum. Social studies curriculum is a hot topic in educational conversations: the choices of what is chosen or excluded from the curriculum can make policymakers, teachers, and parents very uncomfortable.

In the elementary school, social studies, and history, in particular, is often taught as a set of narratives about events that have happened in the world. Teachers rely on materials such as curriculum guides, children's literature, and media (e.g., movies) often to deliver content to students. Much less often, but importantly, teachers also find that newspaper articles and other primary sources can be useful in the teaching of the social studies. More than other areas, documents and texts are often relied on to do the teaching. Inquiry is also a large part of the social studies teaching—in classrooms we have visited of admired teachers, we have seen a board on the wall called an inquiry board, where students post the questions they encounter in their research or studies that they want to continue to pursue. Social studies learning, as much as learning in science, is a process of discovery, comparison, and critical thinking.

When social studies teacher educators talk about teacher preparation in the social studies, they talk about the depth of the content knowledge of teachers as a critical question. How much, and how deeply do teachers need to know about a historical event or a structure in order to engage students in deep learning about the topic? Some would argue that teachers can learn alongside their students in the process of inquiry around a topic; others might counter that a teacher needs to understand different perspectives deeply in order to guide students toward critical engagement with the topic. What we have found in our work with elementary teachers is that there are areas of the social studies curriculum some teachers know quite well and others that grow and develop over time, over years of teaching a topic.

Preservice teachers who are new to the curriculum in your classroom might particularly struggle with their teaching of the social studies. Seeking to position themselves as experts in a classroom is a normal part of a novice teacher's identity work in the classroom. In a recent visit to a preservice teacher's classroom, the preservice teacher read a book about a historical event that impacted over 100,000 Japanese Americans, Japanese internment during World War II. Although the teacher had done background work, when reading the book, a child asked, "Was there adequate food in the camps?" Rather than admit she didn't know, the teacher replied, "Yes, there was adequate food," minimizing the impact of this incarceration on those who were affected. Preservice teachers, as well as all of us, often over-rely on texts that tell one particular narrative of a history or historical event, not considering other perspectives or counternarratives.

One of the more difficult aspects of teaching the social studies is the idea that teachers must adhere to a politically neutral stance in their teaching. Many topics in social studies, from branches of government and the electoral process, to the topic of community helpers, to historical narratives, are not politically neutral topics, but teachers feel pressure to adhere to a neutral stance or to cover all perspectives on an issue. Controversial topics and issues will arise in classroom discussions, and whether and how teachers position themselves in these discussions is an open question, just like the question of the depth of knowledge necessary to teach the social studies is hard to resolve. Many educators would argue that the very idea of neutral teaching is a myth; rather, we always teach what we value or what is valued by schools and society; and that curricular choices are always political. In the social studies, more than any other area, you will have to decide how much of your own perspectives are relevant to classroom discussions; what kinds of models of critical thinking you will provide students, and how far you want to go to push and challenge the idea that teaching can be neutral.

Coaching around Social Studies

In coaching social studies teaching, many of the same issues that come up in teaching will arise in coaching. The first is the content knowledge of the preservice teacher; the second is the choice of materials and practices within the social studies curriculum; and the third is the particular tools and strategies that teachers might draw on to deepen and extend students' thinking.

We know that social studies curriculum is a contested area, and the first challenge for coaches and preservice teachers is the decision of what to address in the curriculum. As we discussed in regards to mathematics coaching, above, we might expect that in the planning of a social studies unit, we might also see a planning meeting in which teachers pore over children's books on a particular historical event and decide in which order they might be shared with students; and to look through websites for primary documents. In doing so, teachers are not only making their decisions about curriculum, but are also deepening their knowledge of a particular domain in the teaching of social studies. Here, as coaches we can address the question of how much, and how deeply do teachers need to know about a historical event or a structure in order to engage students in deep learning about the topic? You may decide that you would like your preservice teacher to study a topic deeply before teaching it, and provide him or her with materials as well as support his or her own quest into the topic. We have often encouraged cooperating teachers to engage in this process alongside the preservice teacher, because we are always learning and deepening our knowledge. When doing so, engage in critical discussions of the different sources and materials gathered, thinking through which materials might also be useful for students inside of the classroom.

This leads us to the second point of coaching, and that is the importance of planning for teaching alongside your preservice teacher. Here, we engage with the question, "How are we designing lessons, how is the structure guiding our students' thinking and disciplinary knowledge?" It is often most difficult for beginning teachers to gauge how a text might interest and engage a student or students in the classroom. Think together about the topic of the text; the text features that might support the student-reader; the way that ideas are constructed and represented in the text; and finally, how the text complements other texts you plan to use in a unit or lesson. It may be worthwhile to create your own rubric when reviewing texts and materials for instruction. How are people represented in the text? Whose perspectives are included and left out? How do students respond to the text, and what are the challenges of the text? These types of guides can be very useful in making decisions about teaching.

Finally, we would like to think with you about the ways that you might engage in coaching around observations of your preservice teacher's teaching in social studies. In post-conferences around social studies teaching, it may be particularly useful to think about how ideas are represented in lessons and how students and teachers together are constructing knowledge and understandings. Let's take, for example, a lesson in which a preservice teacher decided to read aloud the book *Harvesting Hope: The Story of Cesar Chavez* (Krull and Morales, 2003) as part of a lesson on activism. The preservice teacher provided a book introduction before reading the book that guided the students' thinking toward the question, "What are the events in Chavez's life that led to his later activism?" Stopping at different points in the book, the teacher asked students to reflect on injustices and Chavez's responses to those injustices. At the end of the lesson, students were able to come back to the question and provide observations about why a person might choose activism as a path based on their experiences, and the preservice teacher is pleased with the lesson and excited to continue with the next text in the unit. The coach might initially feel a bit unsure of how to engage in coaching around this lesson—the objectives were clear, the book was of high quality and accessible, and the teaching around the book seemed effective. What would you do as a coach? Similar to mathematics coaching, we have to use our coaching practice to more deeply explore the thinking of students across content areas in the classroom. A recording of a class discussion or the artifact of student writing in journals might be helpful here. What often happens in classroom discussions is that the most powerful voices get the most air time in our class discussions. Those voices might even dominate or silence other students in the discussion. We might ask the question, "Who participated, and who was silent?" as a way into a coaching conversation. We might also go the way of ideas, asking, "Who expressed dominant or accepted ways of seeing the topic, and who put forward alternative or less popular responses?" Both of these questions serve to focus our attention on individual students and what we know about their ideas as well as the collective engagement of the class with the topic of study. These questions and observations might potentially lead to conversations about teacher moves that encouraged or widened spaces for multiple perspectives, or ways that the teacher felt challenged in this work.

Teaching and Coaching in Science

Dr. Wendy Saul, The University of Missouri at St. Louis

Teaching Science: Professional Knowledge

Within the Common Core State Standards (CCSS), K-5 science standards are located within the literacy domain—they are integrated into the K-5 reading standards. For example, a teacher might be asked to think about how students are using text features in an informational text or how they are able to communicate in writing the steps or results of a science experiment. Science educators, according to Saul, resist the notion that science should be taught as a part of literacy instruction; and lament the absence of science standards in the CCSS. Often, science educators will turn to sources such as the Next Generation Science Standards (NGSS) (www.nextgenscience.org/). The NGSS have extended the notion of hands-on or inquiry-based science that emerged from the National Science Education Standards (National Research Council [NRC], 1996, 2000) into a set of science practices and core ideas that students will engage with as part of the curriculum. From the NGSS perspective, these practices and core ideas are part of themes that cross subject areas, such as mathematics and engineering, and students are engaged in thinking across areas. Saul explained that our current way of approaching mathematics and science teaching is out of alignment, and often students need mathematical ideas to approach the science curriculum that they have not yet learned, or vice versa.

So, the question of what teachers should know and how they should teach in science is a contested and complex question. As we move into a discussion of professional knowledge in the area of science, we would begin with the statement that like the social studies, science is an area in which elementary teachers often experience both greater autonomy than in other areas, such as literacy and mathematics. Perhaps this has something to do with big tensions in the field. Or maybe there is less emphasis on science because it is left out of the curriculum altogether when schools are focusing on an upcoming high-stakes test. It is also true that curriculum standards are often ambiguous or broad, leaving teachers with great flexibility.

Like social studies, experts ask what we think is the amount of content knowledge that teachers ought to have in science in order to teach effectively. If you are like us, you may have had the experience of being a small step ahead of your students at any given moment around a topic of scientific knowledge such as matter, botany, or arachnids. Children are observers of the natural world and often hold deep knowledge about science that they have built through their observations. Others have engaged deeply in reading or viewing programs about science and have accumulated great knowledge. Teaching science is often, for elementary teachers, an exercise in regaining those skills of observation that we once used regularly. An early childhood professor once commented that very young children will spend the most time peering in a puddle and will repeat the experiment of creating ripples with a rock more often than an older child or adult. Part of science teaching is coming back into that space of wondering about the world and trying to figure out how it works. Of course there are scientific theories and vocabulary that we introduce to children along the way that help them to generalize and make sense of experiences; and it is in this area of articulating ideas about science that teachers often struggle. Dr. Saul explains that rather than pre-teach vocabulary and concepts, science educators will start their work with kids with the hands-on experience and inquiry, and as students make discoveries, teachers will begin to layer vocabulary and big ideas. And within those hands-on experiences, that students will first explore and play with materials before performing more formal experiments. Then, we might picture students adding new vocabulary alongside drawings of experiments in their science journals.

Coaching around Science

Our preservice teachers might find themselves needing to construct content knowledge in science before beginning a new unit of study, and you might come in here to help them build this knowledge in planning conferences or by exploring resources together. Dr. Saul adds that there is an arc or story of science that has been represented over time in trade books and that one part of the preparation might be finding how explanations in science have changed over time or might change across texts. The coach might also work with the preservice teacher to think about how to move beyond trade books to real-world experiences, to engage in inquiry through exploration rather than just through texts.

When looking at videos or student data in post-conferences, we might also think alongside our preservice teacher at the role of the teacher when students are exploring, investigating, writing, talking, and layering ideas and vocabulary into their journals. Just like a teacher in science might engage in co-inquiry with her students, it will be your role to co-investigate teaching alongside your preservice teacher.

Cynthia Ballenger (2009) explains that in the science curriculum, teachers will encounter what she calls "puzzling moments," moments in which students say interesting things that might not reflect traditional knowledge in science. She argues that these moments give us insight into students' thinking, partial understandings, and act as an assessment. However, these moments also are windows into the different ways that students might see the world and help teachers to understand their students' life histories, experiences, and cultures. One of the greatest challenges of teaching in science is to embrace these moments and pursue them, to continue to ponder with students the ideas they're grappling with. Coaching can be a place to examine puzzling moments together and to co-construct understandings of what students are bringing to the classroom.

Teaching and Coaching in Reading
Book Authors

The authors of this book are researchers and teacher educators in the areas of reading and literacy, so we looked within our own content knowledge and PCK to think about coaching in the teaching of reading. When we think about the area of reading instruction, we imagine that it might be an area where you feel a sense of confidence in your teaching. More than any other area, teachers often see themselves as having deep experiences with reading, and often see themselves as readers across genres and contexts. For example, you may not be into novels but you cannot put down the newspaper each morning when you're finished with your coffee. You also read quite a bit as a professional—you read professional articles, curriculum materials, and you read what your students are reading. Because you have these experiences as a reader, you have much to bring to your classroom teaching that will inform your instruction.

Teaching Reading: Professional Knowledge

So what is the knowledge base of teachers of reading? What do you know about reading, reading development, and theories or models of reading? Regardless of your orientation, if you're like us, your teaching of reading reflects your experiences, identity as a reader, and professional knowledge that has been constructed over time and from different sources. You probably also have a model of reading development that you rely upon. Perhaps it is your belief that reading is a social activity, and that readers learn by talking about what they read and making meaning in social groups. Or, you might hold the belief that for the most part, reading is an individual activity—something that happens cognitively, and that students build strategies that they then can apply to new situations. You might see reading as a transaction (Rosenblatt, 1994)—an interaction between the text and the reader that is always unique and constructed in the moment. These models of reading development probably guide what you decide to do in your classroom.

Reading instruction at the elementary level is often focused on both the strategies that readers use when approaching different kinds of texts (e.g., fluency, comprehension strategies, etc.) or mechanics, such as phonics and other structures of language. Vocabulary instruction is a big part of reading curriculum in many classrooms, and if you are a teacher of students who speak a variation of English or multiple languages, you might find yourself teaching vocabulary quite a bit. In addition, you might have a component of your reading instruction that focuses attention on students developing habits of reading, through sustained, self-selected reading time or a reading workshop, perhaps. Your teaching of reading probably crosses content areas, as well, and you probably find yourself teaching reading throughout the school day. Often, elementary teachers have the most coursework and experiences in the teaching of reading—at our own university, we teach three methods courses in the area of literacy, whereas students only have one methods course in other areas.

Beyond the models of reading and methods of instruction, you probably have found that there are practices of teaching reading that are powerful because your district or school or the teachers who you work with have adopted them. These practices usually have an origin or larger community behind them—it might be guided reading, reading workshop, or a curriculum designed by a publishing company. Within these practices, students may choose their own books or the teacher might guide the students in making choices. You probably have a classroom library that provides students with a space to make choices and maybe, a comfortable place to engage in reading.

If you teach in the upper elementary or a departmentalized setting, in which teachers teach the same students different subjects, you may think about reading differently. Or, when you think about the work of reading in a content area like science or social studies, you might draw on a different notion of reading. Reading in the content areas tends to be called "disciplinary" or reading, and may include a greater emphasis on vocabulary or aspects of genre, in particular. For those readers, you may have a bit more work to do as coaches in thinking about coaching preservice teachers to think about reading and reading development within the content area that you are focused upon.

Coaching around Reading

We first thought about Coaching with CARE in the context of literacy teaching when we worked with master teachers to coach one another around their tutoring in a literacy practicum course at our university. Teachers would watch one another teach and then sit together to reflect on the events of the tutoring session. The first thing that we noticed was that these reflection sessions were places in which teachers really articulated and shared their beliefs and models of reading development and revealed what they were bringing in terms of practical knowledge. They talked about the running records of children's oral reading they collected and what they were making of their miscues. They talked about "gaps" in the children's vocabulary that caused the students to struggle in particular texts. And they talked about the brilliance and joy they saw in students when they did a read-aloud that was just perfectly connected to the child's interests or knowledge. This is where we began thinking of coaching with CARE—the ways that teachers engage in their experiences, focused on students, using tools of reflection and critical thought.

It was within the area of reading that we began thinking about Activity Configurations and their role in our coaching, as we previously introduced. Activity Configurations for a read aloud or for a guided reading lesson were useful in our work with coaches who were trying to do the initial work of apprenticing preservice teachers into their practices in the classroom. For example, we found that the preservice teachers were able to access the cooperating teacher's Activity Configuration during the lesson and then it was a shared document for them to talk about together in a post-conference after the preservice teacher observed her cooperating teacher.

Cross-cutting Themes

As elementary teachers, you might find that you are always learning new things about the world and finding ways to share that knowledge with your students, but often in your work you are not seen as an expert in content domains. More and more, teachers are working in departmentalized settings, which shifts this perception of teacher knowledge, but it may still be a tension for you. As you're thinking about your own teaching and your preservice teacher, we would encourage you to think about the expertise you hold in a way that honors and values your knowledge. The importance of an appreciative stance applies to our view of ourselves and others.

There is a tendency in some of these disciplines to represent the content area in distinct knowledge bites (a reductionist curriculum that leads to banking, where teachers are depositing content knowledge through the curriculum rather than approaching learning as a problem-posing process). We heard all of our experts speaking back to this saying to focus on the methods of inquiry in the disciplines, and we found that trend to be both encouraging and aligned with the CARE model. Across the examples we have provided in each of the chapters, our cooperating teachers have shown us that there are far more connections between disciplines than differences, and that coaching addresses issues of curriculum, engagement, and instruction all at once.

Across content areas, we can see that learning to teach in practice comes through looking carefully—being curious—about kids' thinking when engaged in interesting activities. Understanding is not an all-or-nothing, rather, the question is, "In what ways are students understanding _____ in their work today?" You might find this phrase helpful in thinking about the methods of teaching in each content area in your classroom. How does this question look when we are thinking about our teaching in mathematics or writing? In science and social studies?

In terms of coaching and mentoring new teachers, we wonder if there are times that we know our own disciplines so well, and have so much expertise, that our coaching might fall more into the evaluative or directive modes. In other areas, where we might feel less secure, we might engage in more authentic wondering. In our case of collaborative coaching (Chapter 10), when Francine, a cooperating teacher, and Heather, a preservice teacher, showed us how rich the coaching work became when they working together on science/literacy integration. In their year together, they thought deeply about how engagement and equity were related to teaching science and mathematics integrated with ways of knowing and doing from the literacy domains. In coaching, the importance of planning and deepening content knowledge together cannot be emphasized enough. Nor can we say enough how key it is to collect data and puzzle over kids' thinking together and how the post-conference can be a space to both ask questions about participation and engagement, but also to plan together for next steps.

Some Thinking and Talking To Do

- Where do you feel strongest as a teacher, in terms of the content areas we have addressed, and in what areas do you feel your passion has not grown as much? What do you make of those differences?
- When you think about these stronger or less emphasized areas, how does your coaching differ in those areas?
- Just as teaching well involves a great deal of curiosity about student thinking, coaching is the collaborative work of being curious together. In your coaching, how might you have a shared focus on the students' developing understandings?
- When you are coaching, it might be important to collect evidence that will allow you and your preservice teacher to puzzle together about kids' work. Therefore, how will you position both the video camera and the observer to focus on collecting what the kids do?

References

Ballenger, C. (2009). *Puzzling moments, teachable moments: Practicing teacher research in urban classrooms. Practitioners Inquiry Series.* New York, NY: Teachers College Press.

Grossman, P., Compton, C., Igra, D., Ronfeldt, M., Shahan, E., and Williamson, P. (2009). Teaching practice: A cross-professional perspective. *The Teachers College Record, 111*(9), 2055–2100.

Kennedy, M. M. (1999). The role of preservice teacher education. In Darling-Hammond, L. and Sykes, G. *Teaching as the learning profession: Handbook of teaching and policy* (pp. 54–86). San Francisco, CA: Jossey Bass.

Krull, K. and Morales, Y. (2003). *Harvesting hope: The story of Cesar Chavez.* Boston, MA: Houghton Mifflin Harcourt.

Rosenblatt, L. M. (1994). *The reader, the text, the poem: The transactional theory of the literary work.* Carbondale, IL: SIU Press.

Shulman, L. S. (1986). Those who understand: Knowledge growth in teaching. *Educational Researcher, 15*(2), 4–14.

Smith, M. S. and Stein, M. K. (2011). *Five practices for orchestrating productive mathematics discussions.* Reston, VA: National Council of Teachers of Mathematics.

PART IV
Expanding Tools for Coaching

10

COLLABORATIVE COACHING
Building Communities of Practice

We need others to complement and develop our own expertise. This collective character of knowledge does not mean that individuals don't count. In fact, the best communities welcome strong personalities and encourage disagreements and debates. Controversy is part of what makes a community vital, effective, and productive.

(Etienne Wenger, 1998)

The practice turn in teacher education, explained in an earlier chapter, grew out of the study of people learning to do things through affinity, apprenticeship, and increasing degrees of participation. While studies in this area initially focused on the relationship of a mentor to a novice, the focus has more recently shifted to a focus on the qualities of the community of practice (Wenger, 1998). We now turn our attention to the ways in which a teacher education program and a cooperating teacher can build a community that surrounds the development of teaching practices for the preservice teacher. We call this process collaborative coaching, and it is a departure from the status quo separation of the university and school as contexts for teacher preparation.

What we envision is a more collective sense of both what it means to teach and what communities support my development. "What we stand for" is part of our vision. "With whom do I stand?" is a question that taps into the same meaning but in a way that reveals a great deal about the processes of becoming a member of a community. Therefore, in beginning our chapter on collaborative coaching, we reintroduce and explore the notion of visioning in teaching as a collective activity.

Visions and Communities of Practice

We often engage our undergraduates in dialogue around their vision for teaching. The notion of vision, as introduced in Chapter 1, is a very personal construction of why we teach and what we hope for our students (Duffy, 2002). Those who have studied visions in teaching find that our visions are constructed as we have experiences across settings that challenge and confront us with new ways of thinking and knowing about teaching. In our work as teacher educators, as we are continually working to position ourselves, we try to move preservice teachers beyond the notions of why they entered teaching (i.e., "I am great with kids.") to an understanding of their professional lives as contributing to an envisioned society that may be different from the one that exists today. Perhaps this vision is of a society that is more just, more equitable, more opportunity rich for everyone, more peaceful, more cooperative, more democratic, more tolerant, more serving, more present, more appreciative, and more caring.

We know that those we work most closely with in practice shape our visions as a teacher. We learn who we are as a teacher through many associations. Some associations help us to think about what we are not: Consider a preservice teacher placed in a classroom where she finds practices that she or he resists. "I will never do that. I don't believe in that." You may have heard your preservice teacher talk about previous experiences this way. This same teacher will build relationships and find affiliations that lead to more positive statements of identity across the hall, alongside you, or within the community of the preparation program she or he is a part of. When we find others who help us to create a positive vision of who we are as a teacher, we call these affinity groups or communities of practice. Within these groups, we build spaces for our own practices. We practice the language that helps us to express our ideas and name who we are. We learn to articulate what we have come to value in communication with others. We learn the language of a community of practice and thus our membership is solidified.

Communities of practice can become places where visions are enacted and become more powerful. For example, when we are faced with challenges in working toward a particular goal, we draw on shared visions to articulate our obstacles. "We can't become more effective in our writing instruction without longer and more uninterrupted time blocks in the schedule. Let's figure out how we can arrange this." Within communities of practice, strength comes with this clarity of purpose. Often, in the context of gaining power, the community may move from an informal to a formal status. We might give ourselves or be given "a name" that announces who we are to others. "We are the PEACE project teachers, working on creating more positive classrooms in our school."

Communities of practice are essentially collective visions of people working together to teach. Communities that have taken on a practice shape those who enter but are also reshaped by those who enter. A community that thrives often draws on the power of new voices, fresh ideas, and genuine questions.

One of the most common reasons teachers express in taking on a student teacher is that the teacher him or herself will grow and learn. This is not the case of opening a pipeline to new research that pours from the university into classrooms. Rather this growth is the result of reflection that is sparked inside the cooperating teacher and preservice teachers' experiences.

We are part of many communities of practice as teachers. One of the keys to identifying community presence in our lives is found in the use of "we": "In our family, we…"; "In our neighborhood we…"; "In our book club we…." We are a community of authors of this book who share an identity around teacher education. We, including you as readers, are becoming a community of practice around the principles of CARE in supporting others into teaching.

Collaborative Coaching

The Community of Support for the Preservice Teacher

There are multiple communities of support that preservice teachers draw on during their field experience. They draw on their families and friends. They draw on their fellow students in their preparation program. They may draw on faculty in the teacher preparation program. They certainly draw on support through the school community they are part of during their field experiences. Your teaching colleagues are their teaching colleagues. Your administrators are their colleagues. These are all important sources of support that you should work to support and nurture. For this part of the chapter, we are going to focus on the small community of the preservice teacher, the field supervisor, and you as cooperating teacher.

Your preservice teacher is part of a community within his or her teacher preparation program, and you may find that this community initially is a strong support system for him or her. The preservice teacher has course instructors, teaching assistants, and perhaps a field supervisor who will also be guiding him or her in his/her development as a teacher.

Typically, the field supervisor is a former classroom teacher who is assigned to observe the cooperating teacher and evaluate his or her performance. Depending on the institution the field supervisor may be a full faculty member, a clinical or adjunct faculty member, or a graduate student. The preservice teacher may or may not have worked with this person during a previous semester in the program. Typically, the field supervisor is responsible for overseeing the procedures and policies of the university for student teaching, offering or coordinating student teaching seminars, managing relationships with the school and cooperating teacher, observing and giving feedback to the preservice teacher, and assigning the final grade (of pass or fail). Sanaa, a doctoral student who worked with us in our research and development of the CARE model, explained that during her previous experiences as a cooperating teacher, she worked hard to help her preservice teachers get it all "right" when the field supervisor came to visit. She saw her role as helping the teacher to get a good evaluation from the university, but there never were any conversations between the two teacher educators. This is the pattern we seek to disrupt with collaborative coaching.

In our teacher preparation program, the field supervisor's observations of the preservice teacher are part of the state's requirements for certification. The number of observations by the field supervisor may vary from one institution to another but typically there are between three to six formal observations per semester. While there may be informal checking in with the cooperating teacher and perhaps some joint (midterm and end-of-year) conferences with the preservice teacher to discuss progress, that is the extent of the contact in most settings. The tradition is that the field supervisor conducts observations and conferences with the preservice teacher away from the cooperating teacher. Similarly, the cooperating teachers' observations are conducted independent of the field supervisor. Why separate? That is a puzzle. Why not together?

We began with a definition of collaborative coaching as a coaching situation in which the field supervisor, the cooperating teacher, and the preservice teacher meet together to confer about the preservice teacher's teaching and work through the CARE cycle together as a community of practice.

While there has been a general movement in university-based teacher preparation toward more intensive field-experiences, there are some practices that have remained unchanged (Hoffman et al., 2015). First, cooperating teachers carry the bulk of the work in supporting preservice teachers through their practicum experiences. Second, field supervisors carry the responsibility of communicating with the cooperating teachers around program expectations and the supervision (i.e., evaluation) of the performance of the preservice teacher.

The relationship between field supervisors and cooperating teachers is typically cordial, respectful, and professional. Field supervisors conduct a series of formal observations during the student teaching experience in particular. The cooperating teachers have no significant role in these observations. Similarly, cooperating teachers conduct informal observations of their preservice teachers with follow-up debriefing conversations. Typically, the field supervisors have no significant role in these observations. The roles are envisioned as complementary (in support of the preservice teacher) but independent as a function of purpose (e.g., supervision versus coaching). For example, Fayne (2007) asked over 200 preservice teachers to complete a survey assessing the value of the field supervisor in their preparation, and whether they felt there was a distinction between the role of cooperating teacher and field supervisor for them. The preservice teachers positioned the field supervisors as important mentors who "managed the experience, served as confidantes, and made evaluative judgments about performance. Cooperating teachers were viewed as instructional coaches who gave student teachers the physical and psychological space to try out strategies while supporting their efforts with feedback, modeling, and materials" (p. 53). This pattern of work is not, to our knowledge, a result of research that has demonstrated that separate is better but more likely a practice that has emerged out of a combination of convenience, efficiency, and an attempt to respect different roles.

Collaborative Coaching Model

The collaborative coaching model follows the same structure as CARE. The difference is that the field supervisor and the cooperating teacher are both participating in the CARE cycle with the preservice teacher. Instead of working as two teams of two, collaborative coaching makes one strong team of three. Collaborative coaching may not happen in all conferences but over time, it may become the norm. Preservice teachers who have gone through a few cycles initially with just their cooperating teacher or field supervisor are in a better position to participate in the collaborative model.

The Planning Cycle

When we began working with collaborative coaching, the field supervisor and cooperating teacher worked together in the pre-conference, observation, and post-conference. We began to imagine what collaborative coaching might look like in other parts of the coaching cycle, particularly in the planning. We might think of this as collaborative planning (instead of collaborative coaching).

Field supervisors (usually) have many years of teaching experience. Planning can be one of the most complex parts of the teaching cycle. While cooperating and preservice teachers normally engage in this stage of teaching together, the field supervisor's influence could further support the preservice teacher in this process. Moreover, during the planning phase of teaching, the field supervisor might be able, for example, to ask critical questions about the content of the lesson as well as the instructional choices, providing another lens on what the goals and processes are that might be under consideration. We will return to this point in the case at the end of this chapter, but often we have seen extraordinary possibilities when the planning is expanded in collaborative coaching.

The Pre-conference and Observation

The pre-conference, a short conversation, is probably most likely to be a discussion led by the cooperating teacher, but the field supervisor could potentially also take the lead. Returning to our description of the pre-conference in Chapter 6, we would encourage the field supervisor and cooperating teacher to ask the preservice teacher to think about the roles of each person in the observation. The presence of the field supervisor during the observation may free the cooperating teacher to take a greater role in the co-teaching. The addition of another observer could also allow for more small groups to be observed during work time.

During the observation stage of collaborative coaching, you will have to think about ways that the observation can feel more collaborative and less like an audience watching the preservice teacher. If every stage of coaching is aimed at joining efforts in shared attempts to support the pre service teacher, then the observation stage should reflect that spirit as well. While there are realities and necessities to observing the preservice teacher (evaluations, giving preservice teacher space to explore the "lead" teacher role, etc.) we wonder how this stage might feel more collegial and supportive, and less evaluative and performative.

The Post-conference

The post-conference is the space when the most affordances (and challenges) will likely be experienced by the triad. Based on our research we have discovered there are a few key ways that collaborative coaching post-conferences can be designed to be most collaborative and supportive (and not awkward!).

First, although there might be different goals and roles in the conference, it is essential that all participants are informed and part of the shared model for mentoring the preservice teacher—in our case, the CARE model. To build shared understanding, the field supervisor may want to observe through one or more cycles before stepping in as a full participant. Or, if the field supervisor is more experienced with the model, perhaps the roles change, and the cooperating teacher first takes the role of observer. Be sure to build in time to debrief and puzzle over the tricky moments in the conference. Over time, the work can become more collaborative.

Initially, preservice teachers can feel overwhelmed by having two mentors in the conversation, especially if they had a difficult teaching experience. This feeling generally subsides after a couple successful cycles, but talking explicitly about emotions is encouraged. It often works best for one mentor to lead in these more challenging conferences, with the other having a direct role in bringing in data or using coaching language that leads the preservice teacher to say more, to dig deeper. Short preparation meetings between the field supervisor and the cooperating teacher to construct a road map can help.

Space is important. The cooperating teacher and the field supervisor on one side of a table and the preservice teacher on the other is not a good idea. Try a triangle structure and limit the objects between people. Generally, a few printed or written notes or student artifacts will not interfere with eye contact; however, an open laptop can be a barrier to full participation.

One challenge that our coaching teams have had in implementing collaborative coaching is the problem of logistics. Often, our field supervisors oversee 10 or more students in the field, and each one has particular needs in terms of when they are observed and when they can pre- and post-conference. The field supervisors can spend much of their time in communication and scheduling conversations, and at times, this responsibility can take time. When we begin collaborative coaching, we then add the additional task of communicating with the cooperating teacher and finding a time when the three can sit together.

An additional challenge is the potential for mixed messages and role conflicts. Of concern to the preservice teacher can be the difficulty in understanding who has the lead in the conversation. Our experience is that with time, when the CARE model is in action, the preservice teacher comes to see that they are in the driver's seat. The cooperating teacher and university facilitator are there to support the reflection of the preservice teacher, and those role conflicts can subside.

A final area of concern is evaluation. Recall that Sanaa expressed that she saw the field supervisor as the evaluator of the preservice teacher. There is, because of institutional structures, a time when evaluation becomes a reality (e.g., passing, recommendations). It is important to be open and direct around these issues. Both the cooperating teacher and field supervisor will have responsibilities of evaluation, and collaborative coaching opens possibilities for rich conversations about growth and development.

Collaborative coaching is a structure of coaching that asks the triad of the cooperating teacher, field supervisor, and preservice teacher to meet together in a pre- and post-conference around an observation of practice. The potential benefits of this approach are to support the preservice teacher in linking theory and practice, and to avoid positioning the school and university as at odds with each other. From our research, we can also tell that collaborative coaching is an opportunity for growth for both the cooperating teacher as well as the field supervisor, who are both learning and appropriating a new model of coaching. It is a win–win.

A Case: Collaborative Coaching

In the case we present in this chapter, we will share both a bird's eye and close-up view of how collaborative coaching worked in one triad. This case comes from our fourth year working with CARE, and during this year, we had begun our professional development program for cooperating teachers who were not pursuing their master's degree. Francine, a fifth grade, math and science classroom teacher (and graduate student pursuing her master's in literacy) had worked with us the year before in the Master's program, so she was in her second year working with CARE. Francine was also working as a teacher leader in the professional development program; coaching other cooperating teachers. Madeline, a graduate student (pursuing her doctorate in literacy) was the field supervisor but had previously been a cooperating teacher and knew the CARE model from both perspectives—as a cooperating teacher and a field supervisor. Heather, the preservice teacher in a literacy teacher preparation program, had two very experienced mentors.

Francine had decided that even though her classroom was a math/science classroom, that Heather could implement her literacy student teaching work in the classroom. The two decided to experiment with content integration throughout the cycles of CARE they would do in the classroom. Francine reflected in an interview, "I don't know that I would feel brave enough to take it all on alone, as a cooperating teacher." Because of this new challenge, they asked Madeline if she would engage in collaborative coaching throughout the cycles, and even work with them in planning through many of the cycles. Heather agreed, and we decided to study the process as a research project.

During one collaborative coaching cycle Heather planned an integrated science and literature unit, planning with Madeline and Francine separately. This is one model for planning—each coach has a slightly different role in helping the preservice teacher prepare to teach. Heather consulted with Madeline regarding her larger goals of integrating language arts and science, and through the conversations she clarified her big idea of "Stories of the Sky": A unit that disrupted the idea that the science curriculum is the only story of science. Rather, people for thousands of years have been telling other stories about the universe, in spite of scientific discourses that hold power. In collaboration with Francine, Heather worked on selecting texts, organizing hands-on science activities, and gathering materials for the daily teaching. The triad engaged in pre- and post-conferences collaboratively.

In terms of the observation, the triad had to make decisions about each person's role in the teaching. Stemming from Heather's focus on different perspectives represented in children's literature, as she articulated in the pre-conference, Madeline collected data focused on how students were making sense of the literature while she taught the lesson. Francine paid close attention to participation using a critical focus, based on Heather's desire that the students who had histories of being less connected to science might be more engaged by this literature-based approach. Indeed, during and after the post-conference, Heather and Francine found that there had been increased engagement by particularly girls, students of color, English learners (recent refugee students), and students who received interventions. Their shared focus furthered their analysis of how the curriculum shifts were supporting particular students.

Now, we provide a close-up view of what the collaborative coaching looked like in practice within this cycle of coaching. We will focus on the post-conference, as this is where most of the negotiation of turns occurred. Before the interaction we provide here, Francine opened the post-conference with the standard opening: "What have you been thinking about..." and Heather responded that she had been thinking about how surprised she was at how the students responded to the book she chose.

On Francine's road map, she had the intent of thinking with Heather about the language chart, which is a structure Heather was using (with Madeline's support) to record the students' thinking about the books she chose for her literature unit. Francine had noticed that Heather was working hard to "fit" the student responses into the chart she designed. Drawing on her signature coaching move, asking Heather to "slow down the moment," she dove into this tension in teaching.

Heather responded that this book was a little different from the others, which made it "tricky":

> I think the tricky thing with the chart is that this first story [...] it's like in a different vein than stories of the moon from different cultures. When I was thinking about that chart, I was thinking of how the other stories go along with the chart. There's a story and it has some touches of this culture's perspective on this scientific topic—craters in the moon, or seasons, or shadows—and then here's what we know from science about that topic. But then this first one I really couldn't find a book that fit into that same vein so I guess that's just kind of a planning issue, and trying to fit it into something maybe it really didn't fit into. So I don't know. I guess that's what I'm thinking about.

Francine expressed agreement, and then was able to quickly draw on a coaching move, appreciating Heather's strategic teaching moves, with the phrase, "It's really, really complex, like you're juggling so many competing things." Often, during collaborative coaching sessions, Francine's role was to acknowledge and respond in moments when Heather was more likely to critique herself. She read Heather's cues—language such as "So I don't know," as moments when Heather was feeling less confident—and responded by appreciating the difficulty of the work to integrate subject areas.

In a collaborative coaching move, Madeline's speech overlapped with Francine's, and she added, "You took the words right out of my mouth." Sometimes, in collaborative coaching, the two coaches would take this role of supporting one another, sometimes by slightly revoicing what the other said, or other times, offering words of agreement. Often, Francine talked about how positive Madeline's presence was in the coaching conversations, and sometimes, that presence served to support Francine and Heather in the important work they were doing when they reflected together in their practice.

Madeline, who had a greater role in thinking about the ways that Heather might choose literature for her unit and the design of the language chart, brought the post-conference focus back to the ways that Heather was thinking that the language chart might be more relevant in her future lessons. She changed the topic slightly from Francine's talk about the "many competing things" that Heather was "juggling." Madeline, instead, brought the conversation back to a question that Heather asked the students during the lesson about how they thought this kind of "science" work was different for them. Madeline asked, "I think it would be really interesting to see as it progresses, right, like you guys just finished force and motion so if this line of inquiry is through text it's going to be quite different...."

Here, Madeline stepped back and provided a wider lens, bringing attention to the larger scope of the unit.

Francine and Madeline together began to consider how to coach Heather when working with content integration and when fuller participation and learning in the classroom community was the focus. One realization they came to was that Madeline's role would be different from Francine's because often, she might have missed a planning conversation or another teaching experience that was relevant to the discussion. She would use questions to learn more, and in doing so, would often allow space for Heather and Francine to reflect through their narratives of what occurred. What follows is an excerpt from later in the conference, when Madeline took on this coaching role:

> **Francine:** You and I looked at each other, remember you turned the page and some kid did something and you and I looked at each...
>
> **Madeline:** Was this in Block A or B?
>
> **Francine:** In B. I think he said, "ohh" or "wow."
>
> **Heather:** Yeah, it was something like that. There was a lot of I don't know, a ton of interest around the illustrations.
>
> **Madeline:** How did that chatter feel?
>
> **Heather:** (Takes a deep breath) Yeah, I ... I was really trying to get a gauge of whether it was on topic chatter and a lot of it seemed to be. Kids were saying things about the planets and talking about what they knew about it and stuff.

In this interaction, Madeline interrupted a reconstruction of the ways that engagement with the literature was occurring in this classroom with a question about how it felt when there was a lot of chatter amongst the students. Heather, through her response, was able to make an evaluation of how the students were engaged in the discussion or whether the conversation was getting out of hand. She stepped out of the moment to appreciate the learners, and in doing so, affirmed her moves as a teacher by focusing on data.

Madeline's question might have been brief but it was significant in terms of making the familiar strange. It functioned similarly to another coaching move we often heard her use, which was to acknowledge that every teaching move is a choice and in Heather's words in an interview, "When something seems like an obvious choice we talk about what are other choices we have. We often have more freedom than we often give ourselves or think we have." Madeline was able to do this work with Heather and Francine both because of her place as an outsider. She was able to ask about planning and why they chose one book over another; or why the mini-lesson in the unit plan had been replaced by another mini-lesson. Heather made many decisions during the lesson, and Madeline showed great interest in helping Heather to recognize her agency as a teacher.

Although this is not the whole story of how collaborative coaching unfolded in this triad, these brief excerpts show us that collaborative coaching does not mean that both coaches take on the same coaching moves in the conversation. The cooperating teacher will always have the advantage of context and furthermore, will always have the interests of the classroom and the students at the forefront of his or her mind. The field supervisor will be invested in the context but will have the added advantage of his or her outsider status, and ability to ask questions to make the familiar strange. In this triad, over time, those roles became more flexible and at times, it felt as though Heather was so comfortable that the coaches were simply following her lead. As Madeline wrote in a reflection, "I learned from our time together last semester that I did not need detailed notes to talk about. The conference should be led by Heather and her concerns."

Some Thinking and Talking To Do

- Collaborative coaching seems logistically challenging and potentially time-consuming, and your point of contact with the university may not be a steady one. What are some ways you envision the ideas of this chapter—a community of support for preservice teachers—working within your specific context?
- Have you thought about the application of the CARE coaching model in working with other teachers? How would it be similar or different from working with preservice teachers? Easier or harder? Powerful in expanding your community of practice?

References

Duffy, G. G. (2002). Visioning and the development of outstanding teachers. *Literacy Research and Instruction, 41*(4), 331–343.

Fayne, H. R. (2007). Supervision from the student teacher's perspective: An institutional case study. *Studying Teacher Education, 3*(1), 53–66.

Hoffman, J. V., Wetzel, M. M., Maloch, B., Greeter, E., Taylor, L., DeJulio, S., and Vlach, S. K. (2015). What can we learn from studying the coaching interactions between cooperating teachers and preservice teachers? A literature review. *Teaching and Teacher Education, 52*, 99–112.

Wenger, E. (1998). *Communities of practice: Learning, meaning, and identity.* Cambridge, UK: Cambridge University Press.

11

RETROSPECTIVE COACHING ANALYSIS

A Video-based Tool for Coaching

For fast-acting relief, try slowing down.

(Lily Tomlin)

You are becoming a teacher educator, and teacher educators have long been using video to engage preservice teachers to reflect on practice. In this chapter, we will provide an overview of the role of video in Coaching with CARE as well as how video can help you to develop your understandings as a teacher of teachers within a community of coaches.

Grossman and her colleagues (2009) put forward a framework of thinking of teacher preparation that centers on three processes, as we introduced in Chapter 1. The first process is *representations*. In this process, teacher educators put forward models of practice. Much like you did when you asked your preservice teacher to watch you teach in a Purposeful Observation setting, working with representations is an opportunity to see how the teaching goes. Like an Activity Configuration, a representation is a model of a particular activity that we do a lot in our teaching. However, the difference between an Activity Configuration and a representation is that the representation is active and it is observed in action. Beyond what we can understand from reading about practices in books, a representation is enacted. It is a "model lesson" because it represents the component parts of say, a workshop mini-lesson or a science demonstration, but it need not be perfect. In fact, representations should be complex and ripe for conversation.

Representations of practice do not stand alone. Instead, they are accompanied by *deconstructions*—opportunities to interrogate and ask questions about the model lesson. Deconstructions, like the work of the post-conference in the CARE model, ask about moves made in-flight (reflection in action) and afterwards (reflection on action.) Further, we always provide opportunities for approximations and enactments of practice. *Approximations* are the "trying on" of practices, often in more structured spaces, such as teaching to peers or working in a supervised practicum setting. *Enactments* usually refer to the movement of practices in these more structured settings to the natural environment of teaching—the classroom. We will talk about how we think about video across these parts of a practice-based model of learning to teach.

The Use of Video in Teacher Preparation

You may recall video recording your own teaching as a student teacher, and perhaps using that video as the basis for a class discussion or written reflection of your teaching. Or, you may recall viewing videos of practice as part of your teacher preparation or professional development experiences, and then talking with others about what you saw. Video as a tool for teacher learning has a long history in the United States. Initially, researchers used the term "microteaching" (Allen, 1966; Allen and Eve, 1968) to describe the work that teachers would do, teaching a practice lesson with their peers, who assumed the role of high school students. The video became the focus for corrective recommendations about the teacher's practice, but the setting was not truly authentic. Proponents of this approach appreciated the ability to change teaching behaviors without the messiness of real school contexts in the way. The method was widely popularized throughout the late 1960s and early 1970s, when teaching was seen as a set of isolated tasks or behaviors that are learned (often before interacting with "real" students!)

These days, we see that video is used more in terms of a case-based approach. In this model, cases of teaching are used to elicit discussions of teaching practices. In Grossman's (2009) terms, these are representations of practice that can be deconstructed to take more situated views of the complexity of teaching and learning (Shulman, 1992; Sykes and Bird, 1992). Beyond supporting preservice teachers in seeing what teaching "looks like" and "sounds like," representations and deconstructions precede approximations—teaching with peers or in a highly structured environment (Grossman, 2009) and enactments of practice in (real) settings.

In this chapter, you will learn about a third approach to using video, which we call a reflective practice-based use. This shift, again, follows a change in thinking about learning to teach toward a more practice-based, apprenticeship model of teacher preparation with an emphasis on experience and reflection (Grossman and McDonald, 2008). Your use of video will draw from both microteaching (recording teaching of one's own teaching) and case-based video (using videos for the purpose of deconstruction). A reflective practice-based use of video helps us to look at experiences and single moments inside of everyday classroom teaching contexts, and to focus not only on the teacher but on the space where he or she is doing her work. We use video to understand the complexity of classroom teaching (in words and images) but also to provoke spaces for reflective thinking and learning through practice. We want to use video to:

- Document the teaching practices that happen in classrooms.
- Zoom in on particular situations that grab our attention.
- Capture moments of surprise and tension.
- Move from evaluation to rich description in our reflection.
- Find patterns and relationships between teacher moves and learning in classrooms.

Towards these goals, we designed a video tool for mentoring situated within a reflective, strengths-based, appreciative model of coaching, which we discuss below. First, let's talk a little bit about video and the challenges we have using it in our teaching practice.

What Challenges Can I Expect?

Video is not easy for anyone! We don't always love to see our face on screen, and we are often ready to forget an embarrassing teaching moment after it occurs. You may feel very uncomfortable yourself being videotaped. You may count on a twitter of nervous laughter at the beginning of a video-recorded pre- or post-conference, no matter how many times you've videotaped your conferences. Video can be challenging, especially for preservice teachers who already may be experiencing pressure to do well, receive high grades, and be recognized for future job prospects. It our job to help the preservice teacher reduce stress and anxiety about video, and we can suggest a few ways you can facilitate more comfort.

Show Your Own Vulnerability

Ask your preservice teacher to video-record your teaching. Watch it together. Stop the video and talk candidly about what you were thinking ("I didn't know what to say in that moment!" "That was so challenging!")

Use Cases

You might find it easier to find videos of teaching to use as "cases," such as a case of a writing conference, or a case of a teacher leading morning meeting. You might ask your colleagues for videos of their teaching, or look on Vimeo or YouTube. Preview the videos. Be planful: Think about building tools of appreciative language with your preservice teacher to talk about the videos ("Wow, did you see how she just pulled them back to the text?")

Let the Video Move with the Action

Plan ahead for where the camera is placed in the room and how it is focused. You might make a plan after the pre-conference, when you know what the preservice teacher would like to focus on. Think about how to use video to capture the whole classroom, not just the preservice teacher. You may need to zoom in and out, or use the video camera to follow one student or a group through an activity. You can try different moves, such as capturing the teacher from the students' perspective, or vice versa, capturing the students from what would be the teacher's point of view.

Focus on Students in Your Talk

Model student-focused talk when you begin to use video to talk about practice. This focus will make the preservice teacher feel more comfortable (the focus is not on me!) and also will provide a model for using what students are doing as data for reflection.

Provide Choice

Ask your preservice teacher what he or she would feel most comfortable capturing on video. Maybe it is a read-aloud that always seems to go smoothly. Start with places of comfort and then bridge to newer, less comfortable situations, like teaching a small group in math or managing transitions.

Make Time

Allow time for the preservice teacher to view the video alone before using it in an RCA event. You may sacrifice immediacy when you do this, but giving the preservice teacher some time to watch and reflect may take some of the emotions out of video.

It can be useful to use video in a planful way—videotaping classroom events towards focused reflection and coaching, but also to use video to capture things you see happening in the moment that are interesting that you'd like to bring back to your preservice teacher. Now, we will talk more about the formalized practice of Retrospective Coaching Analysis (RCA), an extension of the Coaching with CARE model that brings video into the coaching cycle (see also Mosley Wetzel et al., 2016).

The Evolution of RCA

In your use of the CARE model, you have probably already used videos as a record of the pre-conference, the teaching, and the post-conference. This use of video to support coaching proved to be highly valuable, but we are only scratching the surface using video this way. In our work with the model, cooperating teachers began using their filmed observations of teaching as a part of the post-conference. What we noticed was that those videos became data, just as we use our written notes and photographs and student work as data in the post-conference. We noted that this tool emerged at the moment when the preservice teachers were moving into more independence in their reflective practices, taking more responsibility in planning lessons and making instructional decisions around curriculum, and immersing in problem-solving to meet the needs of a class of learners.

In response to what we learned, we extended the role of video into the post-conference of the coaching cycle. We decided to use "retrospective miscue analysis" (RMA) as proposed by Goodman (1996; 2014) as a model for our work around videos. In RMA, the reader is guided by the teacher in the analysis of reading strategies while listening to an audio recording of his/her oral reading of a text in a previous session.

Goodman (2014) explains: RMA gives readers opportunities to observe and evaluate their responses to written texts. It empowers them to talk about their reading process with knowledgeable readers. And at the same time, RMA provides evaluative evidence for the teacher about the ways readers respond to their own miscues and the texts they read, and shows the degree to which a conscious awareness of miscues influences reading development.

The focus in these RMA sessions is on raising the reader's awareness of strategies they are using in constructing meaning through the text through shared focus on a literacy event. There is an appreciative or "valuing" stance taken in this activity that focuses on the strategies that are working for the reader and can be strengthened further through discussion and analysis. The long-term goal is for the reader to become more active in his or her self-monitoring and in greater control of the range of strategies that can be useful in reaching his/her goals. Similarly, RCA is a process of inquiring into the teaching practices that teachers are using in the name of developing more conscious understanding of teaching moves.

Retrospective Coaching Analysis (RCA)

RCA puts into practice what we believe is most important about learning through experience. It builds on the known as both participants, together, make sense of practice using the tools they have at hand. In the same sense as RMA, the goal is to focus attention on the positive strategies each preservice teacher is using in her teaching—an appreciative stance toward practice. Also similar to RMA, the goals of the cooperating teacher are not to suggest new ideas for teaching but to support preservice teachers to continue to (1) build confidence and take risks in their teaching as well as (2) scaffold independence in reflection as a tool for learning to teach. In other words, the goal of RCA is to practice the act of reflection with a more knowledgeable other.

Types of RCA

We offer you three different types of RCA (Figure 11.1); first is a cooperating teacher-guided session, in which you choose all of the focus points before the post-conference. The second is shared—the preparation is shared and both the cooperating teacher and the preservice teacher come with ideas about focus points, to be negotiated in the post-conference. In the third model, the preservice teacher does the preparation work. No matter which model you choose, it will be your job to observe and record the lesson. Both you and your preservice teacher will review/watch the lesson independently. The difference is in who will choose the focus points for the discussion.

Each session will follow the same procedure as the Coaching with CARE Cycle: planning, or "reflecting for practice;" a pre-conference, "reflecting into practice;" an observation, "reflecting in practice;" and a post-conference, reflecting "on practice." The video comes into the post-conference. We envision the post-conference will go something like this:

1. Begin with the open-ended question that works well for you to begin the conference, such as "What have you been thinking about since you taught?"
2. Consider a road map when choosing points for discussion. Think about how the pre-conference shapes what you will focus on in your points for discussion.
3. Introduce a stopping point with a clear description of why you chose it. This can help to reduce anxiety that the teaching will be criticized. For example, think of saying, "in the pre-conference you asked if I would watch this

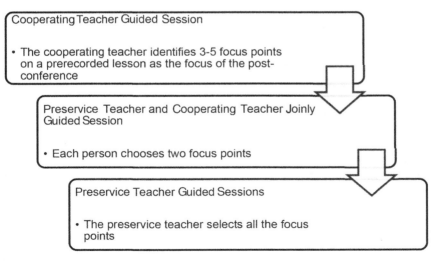

FIGURE 11.1 Three Models of RCA

group of students to see how well they understood this scientific concep so I collected some video of their discussion when they were in small group. Let's watch for what they understand about..."

4. Show the video, but do not start the talk. Let your preservice teacher tak the lead on reflecting on what he or she saw in the video. Ask the preservic teacher to talk through (while pausing the playback) what she was thinking feeling, and attempting to do at that time. Ask probing questions, such a "OK, so what was going through your mind (reflection in action) or what are you thinking right now after seeing that (reflection on action)?"

5. "Watch it again." We cannot emphasize how useful rewatching is to the reflective process. Watch it again with no sound, with a different focus, or jus watch it again. You'll learn new things each time.

6. Make links between each stopping point, focusing on how one relates to the next.

7. Make sure to leave time for talk about how the work of reflection will move you forward in your teaching. Here, use "we" language and think about wha is next for the students. Make a clear action plan for planning, the next step in the reflective cycle.

8. End with a self-evaluation of the process and a plan for the next session (e.g., the lesson, the type of RCA session).

Criteria for Choosing Moments

We find that one of the most challenging aspects of the RCA process is choosing rich moments that are ripe for discussion; we provide the following guideline for your choice. In our work with this practice, we have found that we want to choose moments that will propel us forward in our teaching. We do not wan to choose a moment when things went awry! We want to choose moments tha reveal strategic responses to students using important teaching moves.

We use a four-part framework for analyzing teaching strategies, which we call GLAD: Generative, Learner-focused, Appreciative, and Disruptive. We ask the following questions to analyze what is happening:

How is the moment generative? How will the strategy that I'm seeing in thi moment I'm choosing help me move forward as a literacy teacher? We want to choose moments that have the potential to lead to expansive learning. We are committed to exploring the strategies more deeply and that we have a stake in what we are examining. It is important in reflection to focus our attention on these generative moments.

We ask ourselves a learner-focused question: What is the nature of the young students' engagement and work? We want to focus, in our video, on moments in which learners are doing powerful work, and perhaps, moments when they surprise us or puzzle us with something they say. We are interested in moments when students are really engaged, were building together, and were attending closely to work. Viewing video with the sound off is one way to turn our attention to other ways we know our students are engaged and learning.

We ask questions that are appreciative: What are students doing strategically in this moment? The video is there to help us focus in on a moment and figure out exactly what was powerful. One tool we have to do this is "watch it again." It helps to view a clip multiple times to list the many strategies that students are drawing upon in their work. We also ask appreciative questions about the teaching: What strategy was the teacher using in that moment? For example, maybe your preservice teacher did some reteaching when it was important for a student during a mini-lesson. You ask, "How did you know to do that? What did you gain or lose by making that choice? What are other choices you might have made?"

Finally, we act questions that are critical, or disruptive, such as what was surprising or challenging about this moment? Position yourself as wondering, curious, and authentically interested in the students. These are moments to push on critical issues of power and positioning, as well, such as participation related to gender or language or how particular students are brought into or left out of the action.

GLAD questions are just the entry point, and are not all equal. Figure 11.2 is a visual representation of choosing moments for RCA. The first point being generative, focusing on moments that will lead to growth for both you and your preservice teacher. Often, it is easiest to lead with learner-focused and appreciative moments. Those often lead to moments becoming disruptive, in which they allow space for interrupting the status quo. Just choosing disruptive moments is not a great entry point, because it is important first to recognize and name strategies and then focus on the learner.

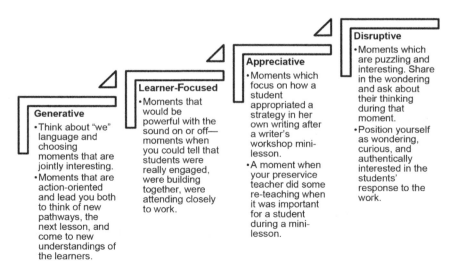

FIGURE 11.2 GLAD: A Guide to Choosing Moments for RCA

Collaborative Coaching and RCA

If you are using this process alongside a field supervisor, we have suggestions for working together to facilitate the RCA process. First, consider an additional planning conference, a pre-RCA conference, after the observation and before the RCA event. This conference will bring you (or your preservice teacher in the case of a preservice teacher or joint-led RCA) and field supervisor to the table together to discuss the event and the stopping points that you are considering. Following the CARE model, the field supervisor might ask you to talk about what you have been thinking about since observing the lesson; your experience of viewing the video; and finally, what moments you hope will spark reflective conversations with the preservice teacher. Planning together for a post-conference can be very powerful.

A Case: RCA

Choosing stopping points was a challenge for the cooperating teachers in each RCA event. Abigail (a cooperating teacher) shared in our first class debriefing event that she had a lot of trouble choosing three video clips:

> So, I picked out a bunch of little clips and I didn't, it's not as neat and clean. [...] I tried to think about what the kids did, and then go back to what she did that influenced that? But even still, I don't know if I really hit this idea of her trying out something that she struggled with and being successful, though I did try to point out things.

It was challenging to decide what kind of moments would encourage reflective conversations, and then to find moments that fit those criteria. Perhaps making a choice of a moment felt limiting to the cooperating teachers, because the choice of a moment guided the conversation in a more directive way than they found in the way they had been coaching up until the point of using RCA.

In making a decision about where to stop, the cooperating teacher was challenged to find a moment that would be appreciative but also would generate learning. Returning to the example above, Abigail explained that it was difficult to freeze a moment without eliciting deficit thought on the part of her preservice teacher:

> So I started by asking her, "What do you see in this?" which I felt a little bit funny about because I didn't know how she was going to take it, and she did, I think she did exactly what I was hoping she wouldn't do. She immediately tried to criticize herself, like, "Well I don't know about this and I don't know about that" and then she started moving into more, I feel like she moved into a little bit more of the positive thinking towards the end of this.

As we cycled through the RCA process two times, the cooperating teachers and preservice teachers became more skilled at choosing moments that became generative and were likely to engage in discussions that focused on their strategies and the students' responses.

Another challenge of RCA was staying with moments of video long enough to engage deeply in reflection on the strategies the preservice teacher brought to her teaching. The cooperating teachers developed a practice that we called, "Let's watch it again," which supported the cooperating teacher and preservice teacher pairs in moving more deeply into reflection around particular moments. Jackie (cooperating teacher) and Monique (preservice teacher) reflected together in the RCA event that when they watched a moment again, they built new understandings:

> **Monique:** [Student's name] had just spoken about how revision was like re-visioning [having a new vision] and I got really excited and said, "Exactly!" The first time I watched it I thought, "Oh no! I just basically told her exactly." But, then when we watched it again, we realized it was actually more co-constructed.

Monique identified that she had used an evaluative word in response to a student. Upon re-watching the video, however, she realized that she and the student were co-constructing an understanding of revision. Here, she was able to move past a self-critique and generate an understanding about her talk with this student. Reflection occurred when the preservice teachers and cooperating teachers were able to stay within certain moments long enough to dig more deeply into what the students were doing and how the teacher's moves were related to the students' work.

Some Thinking and Talking To Do

- How have you used video in your own teaching and reflection on teaching before? What do you bring to this in terms of your emotions?
- Have a conversation with your preservice teacher, asking the same questions.
- Think about when the RCA Model will enhance your coaching work. Do you need to be very comfortable with the process before introducing video, or do you want to make this a part of your coaching from the beginning?
- Draw on the support of the field supervisor for assistance with video-taping and to help you think about moments that were rich and ripe for discussion.
- Videotape your use of RCA with your preservice teacher, and find other coaches to talk with about your practice. You might ask questions like: What was the nature of the talk around these moments? How did carefully chosen

segments of video begin reflective conversations? What kinds of moments were more generative than others in terms of what came next for the preservice teachers' teaching?

References

Allen, D. W. (1966). *Microteaching: A description*. Stanford, CA: Stanford University: School of Education.

Allen, D. W. and Eve, A. W. (1968). Microteaching. *Theory into Practice, 7*(5), 181–185.

Goodman, Y. (1996). Revaluing readers while readers revalue themselves: Retrospective miscue analysis. *Reading Teacher, 49*(8), 600–609.

Goodman, Y. and Marke, A. M. (1996). *Retrospective miscue analysis: Revaluing readers and reading*. New York, NY: Richard C. Owen Publishers.

Goodman, Y. Martens, P. and Flurkey, A. D. (2014). *The essential RMA: A window into readers' thinking*. Katonah, NY: Richard C. Owens Publishing.

Grossman, P., Hammerness, K., and McDonald, M. (2009). Redefining teaching, reimagining teacher education. *Teachers and Teaching: Theory and Practice, 15*(2), 273–289.

Grossman, P. and McDonald, M. (2008). Back to the future: Directions for research in teaching and teacher education. *American Educational Research Journal. 45*(1), 184–205.

Mosley Wetzel, M., Maloch, B., and Hoffman, J. V. (2016). Retrospective video analysis: A reflective tool for teachers and teacher educators. *The Reading Teacher, 70*(5), 533–542.

Shulman, L. (1992). Toward a pedagogy of cases. In J. H. Shulman (Ed.), *Case methods in teacher education* (pp. 1–33). New York, NY: Teachers College Press.

Sykes, G. and Bird, T. (1992). Teacher education and the case idea. *Review of Research in Education, 18*, 457–521.

12
CONCLUSIONS

Coaching with CARE is a pathway to teacher development that has had an enormous impact on our own teacher preparation program as well as the lives of the cooperating teachers we work with. Francine, one of our teachers who leads other cooperating teachers who are learning the CARE model, explained her relationship with her preservice teacher, Heather, as it developed within the CARE framework this way.

> **Interviewer:** What words apply to your relationship?
> **Francine: Love.** She's one of the closest colleagues I teach with. She is the closest. She is so aware of children, but also very committed to troubling these things that we hold on to in schools. It blows me away. I held on very tightly to things that were the status quo, but she (Heather) is committed to wondering. A kid will say something, and she will think, "Whoa," and write it in her notebook. **Admire.** There are only a few teachers who I would feel great if I had a child in their classroom. Heather is one of those teachers.

We are struck by her love and admiration for the preservice teacher who spent one year in her classroom, but what is particularly interesting about Francine's words is the specific naming of Heather's strengths as a teacher in this quote. Heather is committed to wondering and questioning everything. She is a careful observer of students' language. Heather is appreciative and wonders at the brilliance of the students in her room. Without CARE, would Heather have been the same teacher? We cannot say for sure. But we do know that Heather is a teacher who is becoming alongside her mentor, and they both know what is important and relevant to becoming a teacher.

The common development and relationship of the preservice and cooperating teacher is a key component of CARE. One of our favorite artifacts from our time with teachers in the CARE model came to us in an evening session of one of our professional development sessions with cooperating teachers. Towards the end of the year, one of her students drew a picture of the cooperating teacher next to the preservice teacher, with the inscription, "I love my two teachers." As seen in Figure 12.1, the image shows two similarly sized and prominent teachers with the young child, an indication that the child sees both the preservice teacher and the cooperating teachers as teachers.

FIGURE 12.1 Drawing of Cooperating Teacher and Preservice Teacher from a Student

Three Frameworks for CARE

The CARE model is based in a practice view of teacher development. As we introduced in the first chapter and have developed through this book, CARE is based on a few guiding frameworks for thinking about teaching and teacher development. The first is the idea of thoughtfully adaptive teaching (Fairbanks et al., 2009). The framework of thoughtfully adaptive teaching further helps us to explore how teachers might develop through practice-based experiences. Thoughtfully adaptive teachers are able to adapt their practice when new models are introduced or challenges arise to their existing practical knowledge. It is this adaptation that leads to teaching persistence, perseverance, and agency for the teacher who always seeks to learn and grow. We base CARE on the theory that teachers are always adapting their practice in new contexts, and therefore, there is no bank of professional knowledge that will serve a teacher through his or her career. Alternatively, all professional knowledge is tested and reconstructed as teachers adapt to new concepts.

The second framework we introduced and returned to throughout the book is Grossman's (2009) framework for representations, deconstructions, and approximations in practice. In the CARE model, each of these aspects of teaching and learning is represented in the model. Through your development of Activity Configurations and the process of doing Purposeful Observations with your preservice teacher, you engage in these actions of representing and deconstructing practice. We make it clear through our talk and our modeling how we understand the work of teaching within our classroom, and we talk openly about how we are reflecting as teachers on our practice in front of and in display for the preservice teachers we work with. Surrounding every aspect of CARE is also the idea that learning occurs through a process of becoming part of a community of practice, and this framework for learning to teach takes into consideration the importance of apprenticeship and learning through participation, what Rogoff (1995) and others have discussed as the kinds of legitimate participation that novices do as they are becoming part of a set of new practices.

The third framework is the problem-posing approach to preparing teachers (Freire, 1970/1995). A banking model, in contrast, suggests that there is a list of teaching behaviors and ideas that are necessary to acquire for certification or to be hired into teaching positions. We know that there are powerful voices at the national and state level who believe that we can assess teachers' competencies this way. We have to engage in those conversations and show what we know and are able to do in a teacher preparation program to prepare teachers for the work of classroom teaching. However, we hold fast to our view that what prepares strong teachers are multiple opportunities to reflect on teaching and grow their practice alongside others who similarly see teaching as a process of becoming. Freire argued we are always becoming more human as we engage in cycles of problem-posing and problem-solving alongside our communities who have shared goals and purposes. It is the ongoing process of reflection and dialogue that supports our development, not the acquisition of a set of teaching practices.

We do believe that there are specific ways to each discipline that we have to engage in and discover alongside our preservice teachers, and the layers of knowledge we need to support students in their development only continues to unfold as we engage in the CARE model development. In Chapter 9, we share our experience of talking with experts across disciplines about what might be important for coaches to think about across disciplines.

Returning to CARE as a Model

Teachers using the CARE model to mentor and coach preservice and other novice teachers might think of their work as disrupting the status quo of teacher development. The status quo is an evaluative model, in which the goals of the development are compliance to (or movement toward) a model or standard. Rather, in the CARE model, the goal is the construction of a habit of learning through practice using reflection as a professional responsibility. Within both an evaluative model and CARE, there may be varying amounts of expertise. However, in the CARE model, the coaching model emphasizes mutual growth, and the cooperating teachers we work with often comment that their teaching grows as much as their preservice teacher's through the process. As we addressed in Chapter 9, CARE is a model that takes into consideration the knowledge and pedagogies of specific disciplines but also, at its core, focuses the teachers' attention to language, power, and an appreciative view of students and what they bring to the classroom. Often, in evaluative models, the students are not the focus—the attention is on the teacher and his or her actions alone. Reflective coaching in the CARE model tends to introduce tensions in teachers' practices, because of its departure from the status quo. For example, teachers may experience shifts in how they see the roles of the teacher and learner. Often, coaching with CARE subverts more traditional views of curriculum and learning that involves seeing content as separate boxes in a teacher's lesson plan book. Almost always, we hear cooperating teachers comment how when they are observed by their principal or coached by an instructional leader in the school, the differences between the CARE model and the traditional model become even more pronounced. Teachers begin to resist being evaluated using standard assessment protocols and desire a more reflective process for their own professional development. In that sense, tensions arise not only within the teacher but the system that surrounds them. We see these tensions as important and crucial to teachers' growth and development.

Coaching with CARE within a Teacher Preparation Program

We use coaching with CARE across a three-semester teacher preparation program, a Professional Development Sequence, which includes field experiences and courses. The CARE model is infused across what we do in courses and field experiences to prepare preservice teachers for the coaching model we have shared with you in this book. For example, in the first semester, we use CARE as a model for peer observation and feedback. Within a tutorial inside of a reading assessment course, preservice teachers work with a single student and focus with a peer on two big ideas: reflection in and on action (Schön, 1983) as they watch one another and debrief. In the second semester, also in a tutoring context, preservice teachers work with a pair of students with another preservice teacher in a tutoring context and learn to reflect on practice using the CARE model we described in this book. Also, this is the semester when preservice teachers begin their formal internship with cooperating teachers (two days/week). Here, they usually engage in most aspects of the model including Purposeful Observations across content areas and three full cycles of CARE around their own teaching. Cooperating teachers work on developing Activity Configurations during this semester, as well.

In the third semester, which we call student teaching, the preservice teachers continue to use CARE to work with small groups in an integrated classroom based inquiry project. By this time, the reflective practices are in place and they become quite independent in how they are working with the models of peer observation and reflection we've introduced. With their cooperating teachers, they continue to work with CARE cycles and this is when collaborative coaching and RCA seem to find their way into the coaching practice. Again, formally, there are three recorded coaching cycles that the cooperating teacher draws upon for their work in our professional development experience, which we will describe below. However, the CARE cycle begins to encompass more and more of the practices between the cooperating teacher. It is during this semester that we often see preservice teachers begin to "coach themselves" around their practice—leading the pre- and post-conferences in such a way that the cooperating teacher finds freedom to wonder alongside—a position of a co-inquirer, and less of a guide.

A Case: Towards Co-teaching

Amber, cooperating teacher, invited and welcomed Holly, preservice teacher, to take the lead across the coaching cycle throughout their year together. In the final interview, Amber shared,

> That was nice because she [Holly] knew the model. She knew the types of things that I was going to ask or the types of things that we were going to talk about, and she generally picked them up before I did. That was nice because then it was her idea, her observation, and we could dig in and say, if that's something that's interesting to you, what else could we do to facilitate that? Then, again, when it's your idea, you're more willing to take that on. (Final interview, 2014)

The shared knowledge of the CARE model helped both Amber and Holly understand their roles together and independently. Amber knew that her primary role as coach and mentor was to pay close attention to what was important to Holly as a teacher and to help Holly make sense of her thinking through reflecting together.

Amber also recognized that as a coach in the CARE model, there were ideas and practices that she may think are very important in teaching, but rather than trying to mold Holly into the teacher that she is, she aimed to guide Holly to be the teacher that she envisioned for herself.

> Ultimately, it's just back to that same idea that I'm really teaching her how to think and not what to think. There are so many things that I could have taught her from my own experience that she may not ever come into contact with. There may be some things from my experience that she just doesn't agree with, but I've taught her how to think about things, and so when she does come into contact with something new, I think just having the ability to reflect deeply on it, having the ability to know what resources are available and who to turn to and then just that general kind of resourcefulness of finding other options and other possibilities for things.

Amber entered the coaching space with the expectation that there were going to be differences in their focus, ideas, and plans to move forward. Amber recognized that she and Holly were not the same teacher; and therefore, Amber did not seem to struggle with relinquishing control over the students or the classroom. Amber also recognized that Holly had many mentors in her life from family, previous teachers, and the university faculty.

Holly, as a result of learning about the CARE model and agreeing to participate in this model of coaching and mentoring, entered the space as a student teacher who knew that her growth as a teacher depended on her willingness to reflect for, into, in, and on practice. Holly jumped into the process with Amber, and they were off. Holly always recognized Amber as her coach and mentor, and she appreciated the work and space that Amber offered her each day to develop her own practices. In the following excerpt, Holly, like Amber, acknowledged that they were both learning about coaching through the CARE model together:

> I think that I appreciated that it [CARE model] was both new for each of us, and the way of pre-briefing, and then teaching and then debriefing, and that structure, and how the language that we would want to use with each other … And then kind of extend it to, well now I know what she's looking for when she's watching and listening to me. So I felt like it was really constructive that we were both doing it, but now we have much deeper

conversation after the debrief, and I think that that's been really helpful for me to think forward about, what I'm working on and how I'm thinking about moving toward those goals and what she notices that I've done. It is really constructive.

It also seemed like Holly and Amber did not express tensions because they were constantly looking to the future as another opportunity to move forward and try something out again. In other words, they did not believe that any single lesson was permanent. The classroom context, the students, and the teachers were dynamic, and there was always an opportunity to continue today's work tomorrow for both the students and the teachers. Holly explained,

> We just had really great conversations between the things that she was noticing and the things that I was noticing. And kind of being able to plan forward with that, I think I used that as my spring forward to understand the things that she saw me doing, and that I would want to do in the future. (Final interview, 2014)

For Holly, the future meant the work she would do with the kids and Amber, as well as the work she would do when she was the lead teacher in her classroom—and this work was all part of the same process. Holly also took comfort in the knowing that there was time built into the CARE model that was designated time for reflecting with Amber before and after her teaching.

> Because I think before, in general, I just always walk away from a lesson and think, "These are the things that went well, these are the things that I think I need to go forward with," but actually sitting down and following that framework sets up more of a time and space for the mentor and the student teacher, or that's what I felt like for us. That it was a designated time. (Final Interview, 2014)

Holly appreciated the structure of the CARE model, and she felt that the structure became more natural for both herself and Amber. As the year progressed, they knew that they would always plan and debrief before lessons, as well as reflect and plan forward after lessons. Holly identified the space that she was working in as a space to grow. She did not expect to have it all figured out, and in many ways, one reason they may not have explicitly expressed tensions was because they accepted that tensions were part of the process. Teaching is hard work, and it feels hard every day.

> I'm very lucky to have the opportunities to go in and figure out who I was as a teacher. And that's definitely because she made space for me, so as a

reflective teacher she's helped to kind of guide me in the same ways that she thinks ... being reflective to me really means I think thinking about your purpose and considering the best things you're going to do for your students.... (Final Interview, 2014)

Here Holly again established Angela as her "guide." Also, the art of reflection, as Holly saw it, was about adjusting your practice in the best way you can in the moment that you are in right now. And for Holly and Amber, they both knew that by working with the CARE model as their framework, they would have the opportunity again, to sit down again, and work through it all together again.

A Coaching Community

What we have learned is that coaching with CARE is not possible without a caring community of coaches. In our own teacher preparation program, we have worked to develop communities of coaches in two different pathways. First, we developed a master's degree program that focused on mentoring, leadership, and professional development within our university. Teachers applied for the program and were granted a stipend towards tuition and fees associated with the degree program. Over the first year, we gathered in organized courses to introduce and enact the CARE model while a preservice teacher was placed in the room of the master's degree-seeking teacher. Over the following year or two, the teachers completed their degree plan by taking courses in the larger department. The second pathway is a non-degree focused professional development program called the Coaching with CARE Professional Development Program. Also, over a year we work with cooperating teachers and pay them a stipend for their time; but in this case, we see teachers only monthly, not weekly as we do in our master's program (Hoffman et al., 2014; Maloch et al., 2015; Mosley Wetzel et al., 2015).

Working within and across the two pathways, we have learned a great deal about the importance of a community of coaches. Teachers who have worked with CARE have not only appropriated features of the model but also transformed the CARE model in the process. In this final chapter, we will focus on the community building process that we have witnessed. As a community we read together and engaged in conversations around the many dimensions of coaching and mentoring presented in this book.

In our research, we found three functions of the community of practice (COP) of coaches: First, we found the coaches came to deeper conceptual understandings of being a teacher and teacher educator within the COP. Blogging about readings and discussing readings together in class was an important part of developing practices as coaches. In your reading of this book, we hope that you have found a community to work with you to have similar conversations. Secondly, the groups together shared their problems of practice around coaching, working together to think of next steps. At times, that meant being vulnerable and talking about what felt awkward and unproductive. For example, one night, Landon expressed:

> **Landon:** I had my first full experience with like going through the complete coaching process after Amani's first full on lesson by herself, and you know afterwards it's just that, like that state of, "I don't know if I'm doing the right thing. I'm just, I did it.... Hope it's all right!" ... as I was reading the book, I was like, "Well, maybe it's close. Maybe." (Maloch et al., 2015)

The third function, and perhaps the most meaningful work, has been our time in small groups engaged in viewing videos of the CARE cycle. Cooperating teachers bring in their video recordings of their conferences and of teaching, with tagged points in the videos to discuss. The variation in the student teachers, the contexts, and the cooperating teachers themselves led us to rich conversations.

Here is one example of a session "coaching the coach," in which Lanie stopped Jane as she was presenting her video of coaching to ask her about the ways she was questioning her preservice teacher in a pre-conference. Lanie asked, "Pause it. How did you know to ask that question, 'What do you want me to look for?' Whenever she answered, you said, 'How will I know when that's happened?'"

Jane replied, "I asked that because when I was modeling for her that was something I said. I said, 'I know I'll be effective with that mini lesson and conference if I see ...,' and I was real specific, and I wanted to see if she could [get it]."

Landon, making sense of Jane's reply, stated, "So, you almost modeled what she should get out of it." Jane concluded, "Exactly, I modeled for her that out-loud thinking."

As they talked together, the coaches tried to make sense of the kinds of questions that Jane asked, questions that were reflective and responsive to her teacher but not perhaps planned out. As a result, Jane had a chance to articulate her vision of coaching but also her vision of teaching—articulating the ways that evidence from students helps a teacher to know if a lesson was successful. As a result, Landon was able to articulate vision as well, by naming himself what he understood Jane was doing as a coach. This community of practice used the video-debriefing sessions to articulate visions of coaching.

When viewing videos of their coaching as seen in Figure 12.2, the group members practiced the same principles of the CARE model that were applied in the support of the preservice teachers.

We would come together at the end of these small group sessions to report out major insights and challenges. We created out of these sessions both personal and group action plans. We observed in these sessions the growth of the "I am a teacher educator" identity. It grew through shared principles, through practice, and through community. We observed preservice teachers grow at the same time as their cooperating teachers. Everyone drew energy from the process.

FIGURE 12.2 Community of Coaches Sharing Video in a Debriefing Session

Final Thoughts

We are struck by the power of the CARE model as a model for professional development. Although CARE is provided in professional development and university course contexts, we are also able to respond and change with every new year and new group of teachers. We have found, more and more, that the CARE model has changed our own views of teacher preparation and brought us to make changes in our preservice program. For example, we now regularly use peer observation in the CARE cycle when our preservice teachers work in a clinical tutoring experience as part of their reading courses. CARE has become the heart of what we do and how we see teaching and learning to teach.

Each year, we have worked with different communities of teachers engaged in their own professional development, who learn and grow in ways that could not be planned for or anticipated. We have seen teachers using other teachers as a resource in reflecting on their own practices. We have developed the CARE model by watching these teachers work. We didn't read this book. We wrote this book as a community effort.

We hope that you have this same kind of opportunity to participate in a community that is growing through practice. Perhaps there are other cooperating teachers in your school who are working through the CARE model.

We always want to think critically about the communities of practice that surround CARE, and ask, who is included in the community? Who is excluded? And what can we gain by becoming more inclusive? In the fifth year of working with CARE, we began inviting secondary-level teachers into our community. These teachers teach several subjects to several groups of learners each and every day, and have 160 instead of 20 students in their care. Their coaching is qualitatively different from our elementary teachers. However, what we began to see is that they had developed tools as cooperating teachers that we learned from. "This period, you'll watch me, and then next time, you'll lead that activity." Intermediate elementary teachers learned from this practice and began to think about how they might coach differently in their departmentalized contexts. As you participate in communities of practice, it is always important to reflect on those who are outside of the community, and how would their inclusion strengthens the larger community of practice?

You are now part of the CARE community of teachers who are committed to their work as teacher educators. We will return to the question, "You are a teacher educator. How does that sound?" We will ask that you continue to engage with us and others about your work, and consider the ways that our community can extend.

References

Hoffman, J.V., Mosley Wetzel, M., Maloch, B., Taylor, L., Adonyi Pruitt, A., Greeter, E. and Vlach, S. K. (2014). Cooperating teachers coaching preservice teachers around literacy practices: A design/development study of coaching with CARE. *63rd Yearbook of the Literacy Research Association,* 199–215.

Mosley Wetzel, M., Maloch, B., Hoffman, J.V., Taylor, L. A., Vlach, S. K., and Greeter, E. (2015). Developing mentoring practices through video-focused responsive discourse analysis. *Literacy Research: Theory, Method, and Practice,* 64(1), 359–378.

Maloch, B., Mosley Wetzel, M., Hoffman, J.V., Taylor, L. A., Adonyi Pruitt, A., Vlach, S. K., and Greeter, E. (2015). The appropriation of the coaching with CARE model with preservice teachers the role of community. *Literacy Research: Theory, Method, and Practice,* 64(1), 339–358.

Rogoff, B. (1995). Observing sociocultural activity on three planes: Participatory appropriation, guided participation, and apprenticeship. In J.V. Wertsch, P. del Rio, and A. Alvarez (Eds.), *Sociocultural studies of mind* (pp. 139–164). Cambridge, UK: Cambridge University Press.

Schön, D. A. (1983). *The reflective practitioner: How professionals think in action.* New York, NY: Basic Books.

APPENDIX A

READ-ALOUD PRACTICE FRAMEWORK

Activity Configurations

An Activity Configuration consists of:

Products. What is the work being produced? How does this challenge the known? **and** Why are we doing this work? (learning outcomes)

Critical Components. What should be present in the activity?

Optional Components. What enhances the activity but may not always be present?

Variations. The range of possibilities of components from not acceptable to acceptable to optimal.

Activity Configuration: Read-aloud

Outcomes (Products): To create a representation of our personal and shared understanding and appreciation of a valuable piece of literature that challenges prior knowledge, beliefs, and values.

Learning Outcomes: Comprehension, vocabulary, appreciation.

Required Critical Components	Unacceptable	Acceptable	Optimal
Book Selection	Questionable literary quality. Unrelated to student interests with few potential links to other curricular areas. Mostly disconnected from other books we have been and will be using in the read-aloud. So demanding (in terms of accessibility) that most of the kids in the class could not choose the book to read as part of independent reading. Will not likely evoke an aesthetic response from the students.	High quality literature. Related to student interests and with at least potential links to at least one other curriculum area. Connected thematically (or in other ways) to books read before or to books that will be read. A level of accessibility that most of the students in the class could be successful with the book in a reader's workshop setting. Will likely evoke a strong aesthetic response from the students. The text should challenge prior knowledge, beliefs, and values.	Acceptable qualities, AND book is likely to become an anchor text for work that is done throughout the year in writing and work in other areas. Book is likely to spark students' imagination and curiosity toward inquiry projects and multi-model response activities both in school and out of school.
Teacher Expression	The oral reading of the text is flat and lifeless. The volume is not at a level the students can hear.	The teacher is highly expressive in the reading of the text with appropriate volume and articulation. The author's words are prominent, in the foreground, and carry the momentum of the experience.	The teacher is (appropriately) dramatic in the reading of the text (e.g., with character voices, props, movement.)
Student Talk	None or minimal amount of student talk in pre/during/or post reading. Student talk is limited to mostly direct responses to teacher questions.	Students are given opportunities (at appropriate times) to talk in response to the text using pair-share, think-alouds, and student initiated responses. Student talk is limited and does not detract from the rhythm of the text being read.	Acceptable qualities AND a high level of student initiated responses.

(continued)

Required Critical Components	Unacceptable	Acceptable	Optimal
Teacher Talk	None or minimal amount of teacher talk in pre/during/or post reading. Teacher talk is limited to direct questioning of students. On the opposite extreme, there is so much teacher talk that the rhythm of the text is disrupted.	Teacher is explicit about why the book has been selected for the read aloud. Teacher may activate prior knowledge as needed before or during reading. Teacher mostly models thinking during the read-aloud and invites students to do the same. Teacher talk is at important junctures in the text and does not detract from the rhythm of the text being read. If students have copies of the text (e.g., in a "read-along" setting) then the teacher incorporates this access into the discussion (e.g., let's look at what the author says here).	Acceptable AND teacher may focus on particular comprehension strategies (e.g., imagery) as part of the think-aloud processes. There is explicit explanation of the strategy before reading with a reminder for application in independent reading. Attention to the strategy does not become foregrounded. The text meaning stays prominent.
Images (for texts with illustrations)	Images are not used to enhance the meaning construction with the students. Illustrations are simple "shown"/displayed for the students to look at.	Images are actively used to construct meaning. Images are used to evoke responses and nuances of the meaning of the text, including informational text with charts, diagrams, and graphs.	Acceptable AND images are explicitly examined for the ways in which the illustrator (both stylistically and in the composition of the illustration) extends the author's words.
Vocabulary	No explicit attention to vocabulary (word meanings).	Attention to developing word meanings is part of the read aloud experience. Teacher is selective in the focus on words so as not to overwhelm the reading.	Acceptable AND words are gathered, organized for study and use in the classroom.

	Unacceptable	Acceptable	Optimal
Response: Text/Literate Environment	No texts are created as part of the interaction with the read-aloud book.	Texts are created, organized, and displayed in a way that values students' active construction of meaning (e.g., response journals, sketches, vocabulary charts).	Acceptable AND students may take the ideas, structures, craft elements of the text into their own writing.
Frequency/Time	Twice or less than twice a week with sessions at less than 25 minutes.	Three or four days per week with sessions lasting more than 25 minutes.	Acceptable AND every day.
Management of Time and Space	Students are not in a comfortable space, cannot see or hear, and/or do not have a clear understanding of acceptable participation.	Students are comfortable (at their desks or in a group). They can see and hear. There are clear expectations for patterns of participation.	Acceptable AND teacher creates a space where students can see both the teacher, the text and each other (to facilitate discussion).
Optional Components	**Unacceptable**	**Acceptable**	**Optimal**
Curriculum Connections	No curriculum connections are made.	"…and even TEKS" with "and state or district standards."	Acceptable AND explicit connections to curriculum outcomes in other areas (e.g., social studies, writing).
Writing/Craft Connections	No craft connections are made.	Teacher brings the craft elements from the read-aloud into the teaching of writing.	Acceptable AND teacher may use the read-aloud as the basis for genre writing lessons.
Readers' Theater	No connections to drama.	Teacher incorporates readers' theater (and other forms of dramatic activity) into the read-aloud.	Acceptable AND readers' theater and other forms of dramatic activity are incorporated into response activities.

(continued)

Optional Components	Unacceptable	Acceptable	Optimal
Inquiry	No inquiry.	Teacher uses the context of the text and student "wonderings" as the basis for research that is brought back into the discussion of the read-aloud.	Acceptable AND full inquiry projects flow out of the read-aloud. The inquiry projects may be individual, small group, whole-class, or a combination of the above.
Complementary Texts	No other texts are displayed or discussed or used in relation to the read-aloud.	Teacher displays a collection of complementary texts that may related thematically to the read-aloud in an attractive manner and provides access to these other texts for the students to engage with in independent reading.	Acceptable AND the complementary texts are available for students to check out for a home reading. Response and opportunities for students to share their responses to these texts are provided.

APPENDIX B

SUBJECT AREA OR PRACTICE FRAMEWORK

Activity Configurations

An Activity Configuration consists of:

Products. What is the work being produced? How does this challenge the known? **and** Why are we doing this work? (learning outcomes)

Critical Components. What should be present in the activity?

Optional Components. What enhances the activity but may not always be present?

Variations. Range of possibilities of components from not acceptable to acceptable to optimal.

Activity Configuration

Outcomes (Products):

Required Critical Components	Unacceptable	Acceptable	Optimal
Optional Components	Unacceptable	Acceptable	Optimal

APPENDIX C
PURPOSEFUL OBSERVATION

*Areas to record data which serve as a record.
Student Teacher/Intern:
Cooperating Teacher:
Date of Observation: **Start Time:**   **End Time:**
Subject Observed:

Pre-conference (Led by ST)

What are you working on today with the students?

Briefly talk me through what you'll be doing today.

What do you expect will be challenging for the students?

What would you like me to focus on, relating to the students, in my observation?

What should my role be in the activity?

*Notes from the pre-conference:

Observation

Direct Observation	*Reflections and Questions*

*Focus (from the pre-conference):

Post-conference (Led by ST)

Attention should be paid to positive language that is non-evaluative (avoid "I liked when..." and *instead use*, "I noticed that when you ... the students responded...").

What have you been thinking about since you taught the lesson? (You as the CT may come with a set of bullet points of what you've been thinking of.)

What was challenging for the students?

What surprised you?

What changes or adjustments did you make while you were teaching?

What are you thinking about changing next time?

What else is on your mind?

Reflection on Purposeful Observation (Independent Reflection)

*Below are some of the key points from our post-observation conference.

*How was going through this process?

*What did you learn? What will you take with you moving forward?

APPENDIX D
STUDENT TEACHER PACING GUIDE
All Subject Area Classroom

Pacing guides map out the plans for the preservice teacher's involvement. Pacing guides can be constructed at the beginning of a semester and then adjusted as needed. These two example pacing guides show when preservice teachers are co-teaching or observing with cooperating teachers (blank), teaching with the cooperating teacher's plans (light grey), and teaching with own plans (dark grey). The examples are for classrooms in which the teachers teach all subjects and classrooms that are departmentalized, in which case the same lesson may be repeated. Of course, your pacing guide will be tailored to your unique setting.

Preservice Teacher Name: _____

Room: _____

School: _____

Grade: _____

Cooperating Teacher: _____

Semester: _____

Area→	Procedures, Transitions and Energizers	SSR/ Planners	Reading	Writing	Science/ Social Studies	Math (3rd Grade)	Read-Aloud	Library/ Technology (3rd)
Time →	Varies	7:45–8:15	8:15–9:30	10:00–10:45 Spelling M/F	10:50–11:30	1:00–2:30	2:30–2:45	7:45–8:30 Tuesday/ Thursday
Week ↓								
Date								
2/10 1								
2/17 2								
2/24 3								
3/3 4								
	SPRING BREAK!							
3/17 5								
3/24 6								

Date	Week								Legend
3/31 (M/Th/F)	7								
4/7	8								
4/14	9								
4/21	10								
4/28	11								
							PT teach using own plans	Blank	Observation/co-teaching
PT Teach Using CT Plans									

Student Teacher Pacing Guide
Departmentalized Classroom

Preservice Teacher Name: _____
Room: _____

School: _____
Grade: _____

Cooperating Teacher: _____
Semester: _____

Subject →	Beginning of Day	Language Arts	Social Studies	Homeroom		Math	Science
Time →		Block A Block B	9:00–11:00 12:10–2:10	2:10–3:00			
Week →							
Date							
1 2/15							
2 2/22 (No Friday)							
3 2/29 (No Friday)							
4 3/7							
5 3/14	SPRING BREAK						
6 3/21							
7 3/28 (No M/F)							

		ST w/ CT's plans	ST w/ own plans	Co-teaching	Total Teach		
4/4	8						
4/11	9						
4/18 (No Friday)	10						
4/25	11						
5/2	12						
Key		ST w/ CT's plans	ST w/ own plans	Co-teaching	Total Teach		

APPENDIX E

CREATING COACHING CYCLE VIDEOS FOR PC AND MAC

Creating Coaching Cycle Videos (Mac)

Recording Videos

- For Webcam:
  a. Open QuickTime Player and go to "File" → "New Movie Recording."
  b. Click the red button to start recording, and click it again to stop recording.
- For Smartphone, Tablet, or Video Camera:
  a. Record the video using your preferred device and connect that device to your computer.
  b. Open QuickTime Player, go to "File" → "Open File."
  c. Locate your video file on your computer and click "Open".

Note: Record and save each part of the lesson cycle (pre-conference, observation, post-conference, in a separate video file.

Saving/Compressing Videos

1. In QuickTime Player, go to "File" → "Export" → "480p."
2. Rename the file (see *Naming Videos* below), select the location you want it to save, and click "Save."

Note: This exporting step is important because it compresses the file size. This will make it easier for you to upload (as well as save space on your computer).

Naming Videos

- Name each file in the following way:
  - LASTNAME_CYCLE (ABBREVIATION and NUMBER)_DATE (MM.DD.YY)
  - For example, if Jane Doe recorded her first pre-conference on October 24, 2014 the video would be named: DOE_PRE1_10.24.14.
  - If you have multiple videos for a particular part of the lesson cycle (e.g., you have three different video clips from the lesson observation), you can use letters to differentiate them: OBS1a, OBS1b, etc.
- You can use the following abbreviations for the lesson cycle: PRE (Pre-conference), OBS (Observation), and POST (Post-conference).

Creating Coaching Cycle Videos (PC)

Recording Videos

- For Webcam
  a. Open Movie Maker and select "Webcam video" at the top left of the screen.
  b. Click the red button to start recording, and click it again to stop recording.
- For Smartphone, Tablet, or Video Camera:
  a. Record the video using your preferred device and connect that device to your computer.
  b. Open Movie Maker and select "Add videos and photos."
  c. Find your video file on your computer and click "Open."

Note: Record and save each part of the lesson cycle (pre-conference, observation, post-conference) in a separate video file.

Saving/Compressing Videos

1. In Movie Maker, go to the Notebook icon next to the "Home" tab at the top left of the screen, and select "Save movie" → "For computer."
2. Rename the file (see *Naming Videos* below), select the location you want it to save, and click "Save."

Note: This step is important because it compresses the file size. This will make it easier for you to upload (as well as save space on your computer).

Naming Videos

- Name each file in the following way:
    - LASTNAME_CYCLE (ABBREVIATION and NUMBER)_DATE (MM.DD.YY)
    - For example, if Jane Doe recorded her first preconference on October 24, 2014 the video would be named: DOE_PRE1_10.24.14 .
    - If you have multiple videos for a particular part of the lesson cycle (e.g., you have three different video clips from the lesson observation), you can use letters to differentiate them: OBS1a, OBS1b, etc.
- You can use the following abbreviations for the lesson cycle: PRE (Pre-conference), OBS (Observation), and POST (Post-conference).

APPENDIX F

TEACHING PERFORMANCE ASSESSMENT

Parent/Guardian Permission Letter

Dear Parent/Guardian:

This semester your child's class is working with (preservice teacher name), a preservice teacher from (university name). Hosting a preservice teacher is an opportunity to develop mentorship skills that will benefit my practice as a teacher, the preservice teacher's practice, and the students of our class. To support this work, I will occasionally video-record our preservice teacher's teaching. Although the video will show both the preservice teacher and various students, the main focus is on the preservice teacher, not the students in the class. To support our work, samples of student work will be collected as evidence of learning. I will only use the videotape and work samples for the purpose of mentorship activities (conferences with the preservice teacher and other teacher's working on their mentorship skills). Student names will be removed from all submitted materials, and all materials will be kept confidential.

Please complete and return this form to document your permission for these activities. If you have any questions, please contact (principal name and phone number), (your name and phone number), or (the university supervisor's name and phone number) from (university name) who oversees the preservice teachers at this school site.

Sincerely,

Classroom Teacher Name

PERMISSION FORM

Student Name _____

School/Teacher _____

I am the parent/legal guardian of the student named above. I have received and read your letter regarding the (university name) preservice teacher in my child's classroom and agree to the following:

(Please check the appropriate blank below.)

_____ **I DO** give permission for my child to appear on the video and have their work included with their name removed.

_____ **I DO NOT** give permission for my child to appear on the video recording, and understand that he/she will be seated outside of the recorded activities.

_____   _____
Signature of Parent or Guardian   Date

_____
Print Name of Parent or Guardian

ABOUT THE AUTHORS

The authors of this text are former classroom teachers who are all active in the field-based teacher preparation program in the College of Education at The University of Texas at Austin.

Melissa Mosley Wetzel is Associate Professor of Language and Literacy in the Department of Curriculum and Instruction at The University of Texas at Austin. Her research and teaching focus on how preservice teachers construct critical literacy and culturally relevant practices within field-based literacy teaching experiences, as well as the mentoring and coaching of preservice teachers. She is the co-author with Rebecca Rogers of the book *Designing Critical Literacy Education through Critical Discourse Analysis: Pedagogical and Research Tools for Teacher-Researchers* (Routledge). Email: mmwetzel@utexas.edu

James V. Hoffman is Professor of Language and Literacy Studies in the Department of Curriculum and Instruction at The University of Texas at Austin. His research interests include preservice teacher education, international development in literacy, and classroom teaching of literacy. Email: jhoffman@austin.utexas.edu

Beth Maloch is Professor of Language and Literacy Studies in the Department of Curriculum and Instruction and Associate Dean of Teacher Education, Student Affairs, and Administration for the College of Education at The University of Texas at Austin. Her research interests include preservice teacher education, how teachers and students make use of informational texts, and literature discussion. She teaches undergraduate courses in literacy methods and graduate courses in classroom discourse and discourse analysis. Email: bmaloch@austin.utexas.edu

INDEX

Made in United States
North Haven, CT
08 August 2024

55854922R00108